CH

D0015939

DISCARD

OCT   2016

Westminster Public Library
3705 W. 112th Ave.
Westminster, CO 80031
www.westminsterlibrary.org

Finally, my good friend Bill Purvis has put his amazing life story into print! I encouraged him to do this years ago. Bill's story of how he turned his mess into his message will hold your attention to the very last page. Read the first chapter and you'll be hooked! You'll want to put this into the hands of anyone needing an encouraging message that life-change is possible!

John C. Maxwell, bestselling *New York Times* author and leadership expert

This book is *long* overdue! Bill has been a friend and encourager to me for years, and his story is a true testament to what God can do in your life, from wherever you start. Each chapter will challenge and raise your faith, which is what you want a book to do. *Make a Break for It* delivers!

Tim Hudson, 2014 World Series Champion pitcher, San Francisco Giants, four times All Star

In today's world, with all the challenges we face, Bill's words of wisdom and encouragement on how to live your life are very inspirational. Live your life for God, being good to others . . . this book is right on the mark.

Bill Jordan, CEO, President and Founder of Jordan Outdoor Enterprises and Realtree Camouflage

I have had the privilege of having a friendship that spans thirty years with Dr. Bill Purvis, so it gives me great joy to recommend his book, *Make a Break for It*. Bill goes into great detail to tell you how he broke away from a lifestyle that appealed to his lowest and least and how he responded to a new lifestyle that has brought him to his highest and best. This is the type of book that can help transform a person's life not only on this earth, but for all of eternity. If I had a friend who needed to turn his life around, this is the book that I would recommend. My advice to you is to "make a break for it" and get to your local bookstore as soon as possible!

Dr. Dwight "Ike" Reighard, Senior Pastor, Piedmont Church

Bill will remind you of the often overlooked yet powerful ability that God has given us: the power to choose! Choosing to live your life intentionally and purposefully is one of the most important decisions you can make. Bill is living proof of that, and his testimony inspires hope while his words ignite passion to continually pursue God's plan for your life. No matter what trails behind you from yesterday or lies in front of you today, you can, "make a break for it", and watch God truly bless your future!

Chasity Hardman Smith, Miss Georgia 2008
and First Runner-up, Miss America 2009

This book is a game changer! Make a break for it!

Frank Shamrock, Five-Time UFC World Champion,
author of *Uncaged: My Life as a Champion MMA Fighter*

Make a Break for It will change your life! Our strength lies in our ability to overcome obstacles. Bill is a living example of someone who overcame enormous obstacles. Using his dramatic testimony, he shows readers they too can overcome any obstacle in their life though God's power!

Bill Kazmaier, Three-time World's Strongest Man,
Powerlifter and Wrestler

MAKE
A BREAK
FOR IT

MAKE
A BREAK
FOR IT

---

*Unleashing the Power of Personal
and Spiritual Growth*

BILL PURVIS

ZONDERVAN

Make a Break for It
Copyright © 2016 by Bill Purvis

Requests for information should be addressed to:
Zondervan, 3900 *Sparks Dr. SE, Grand Rapids, Michigan* 49546

ISBN 978-0310-34354-7 (ebook)

Library of Congress Cataloging-in-Publication Data

Names: Purvis, Bill (Pastor) author.
Title: Make a break for it : unleashing the power of personal and spiritual growth / by Bill
    Purvis.
Description: Grand Rapids : Zondervan, 2016. | Includes bibliographical references.
Identifiers: LCCN 2015040813 | ISBN 9780310343530 (hardcover)
Subjects: LCSH: Purvis, Bill (Pastor) | Converts--United States--Biography.
Classification: LCC BV4935.P86 A3 2016 | DDC 277.3/082092--dc23 LC record available at
    http://lccn.loc.gov/2015040813

Scripture quotations are taken from New American Standard Bible® (NASB). Copyright ©
1960, 1962, 1963, 1968, 1971, 1972, 1973, 1975, 1977, 1995 by The Lockman Foundation. Used by
permission. (www.Lockman.org)

Any Internet addresses (websites, blogs, etc.) and telephone numbers in this book are
offered as a resource. They are not intended in any way to be or imply an endorsement by
Zondervan, nor does Zondervan vouch for the content of these sites and numbers for the life
of this book.

All rights reserved. No part of this publication may be reproduced, stored in a retrieval
system, or transmitted in any form or by any means—electronic, mechanical, photocopy,
recording, or any other—except for brief quotations in printed reviews, without the prior
permission of the publisher.

Published in association with Dupree/Miller & Associates, Inc., 100 Highland Park Village,
Suite 350, Dallas, TX 75205.

Cover design: Dual Identity
Cover photos: © alexsvirid / © xpixels / Shutterstock®
Interior design: Kait Lamphere

First Printing January 2016/Printed in the United States of America

Contents

Acknowledgments

I am beyond excited to be a part of the Zondervan family and to have had the privilege of working with my editor, Sandy Vander Zicht. Sandy, I am so grateful for your passion for excellence and your editorial insight through each phase of this project. You and your team have been a pleasure to work with.

Without my literary agent, Nena Madonia-Oshman, this book would not exist. Nena, I know beyond a shadow of a doubt that God ordained our meeting, and I am incredibly grateful for your guidance and belief in me. From the start, you believed this book could have an impact, and you worked as if it were your sole mission to see it come about. *Thank you.* I will forever be grateful to you and Dupree/Miller & Associates for believing in my story.

I can't say enough about James (Jim) Lund. Jim, your writing and editing expertise are remarkable. Just as a great chef can take basic ingredients and turn them into an amazing dish, you turned my everyday stories and ideas into an amazing and meaningful book. I love your spirit and am glad this project brought us together.

I don't have enough space to say all that's on my heart to my wife, Debbie. Debbie, you have loved me and pushed me to pursue every dream. I am the most blessed man I know because of you. Thank you for sharing your life with me. You've made life fun!

I am grateful to my firstborn son, B.J. Seven years ago you, B.J., decided that my story needed to be told, and you made it your mission to get it to print. Thank you for continuing to believe in this book, even when it seemed like it would never come to fruition. Thank you for handling all of the small details that have popped up since this project began. Your focus and drive have kept me on track throughout this entire process. I admire you, B.J., and have loved going on this book-writing journey with you!

To my son Brent, incredible copastor with me, thanks for leading so well and freeing me up so I could do this work.

I'm thankful to my son Blake. Blake, thank you for using your flying skills to take me to speaking engagements. Because of you, I met some awesome people whose stories ended up in the pages of this book.

My heart is full of gratitude for our Cascade Hills Church family in Columbus, Georgia. I could have filled a hundred books with stories of our journey together. While you know I believe in you and I've taught you, what you might not know is that you have taught me also. You've shaped my life, and you've believed in me when I've needed it most. I love you.

I'm grateful most of all to God. If He had not sent His Son, Jesus, to die for my sins, I wouldn't be here today. He took an aimless teenager heading down the wrong path and saved him. God turned a traumatic night into a triumphant one. He had a plan and purpose for my life that was far greater than I ever could have imagined. I will forever thank Him for saving my life that night, but most of all, I'm grateful for what He did on the cross for me. I trust this book will give hope and inspiration to those who are looking for it. If God can save me from a life of despair, He can do the same for you.

Introduction

Do you ever feel as if your whole life is stuck in a traffic jam, on idle as you wait . . . and wait . . . and then wait some more for a lane to open up so you can get on the fast track to where you want to be? Or maybe you feel more like you're in a roundabout. You keep going around in circles, driving past one exit after another because you don't have any idea where you're supposed to go next.

If so, I understand how you feel. In fact, that's precisely what I experienced the first seventeen years of my life. I had no sense of purpose or direction. Deep down, I sensed that there had to be more to life, but I sure didn't know what "more" could be. I was aimless. Drifting. Reckless.

That combination of recklessness and wanting more is what led me to a near-fatal encounter with a prostitute one night. What I expected to be a new thrill in my otherwise unsatisfying life suddenly turned into something else—robbery and attempted murder. I was stabbed three times and should have died. I *would* have, except that God heard my desperate prayer and spared my pathetic life. He took a boy with a dysfunctional past and showed him how to break through to a dynamic future. My life has not been the same since.

Before that fateful night, I was the last guy in the world who thought he would see and enjoy incredible adventures with God. I spent my time on the lake, working, hanging out, and in pool halls, but never in a church pew. I'd been rejected by my father and wasted my weekends on carousing. If you had told me at seventeen that I would one day become a happily married husband, devoted father, and pastor of a church with eight thousand members, I'd have laughed in your face. Not a chance! But that was exactly the plan God had for me. And once I gave Him control of my life, He showed me how to break down barriers, overcome my aimlessness, live out my faith, and step into a surprising and fulfilling future.

I believe with all my heart that God desires to do the very same for you. He loves you as His unique creation, as one of His very own children—because that is exactly what and who you are. Do you feel trapped by the mundane or yearn for significance? Is there a dream hidden deep inside of you that you've never dared to voice? Do you feel that you were made for more than the life you're living now, yet don't know how to find it? God understands those frustrations and desires because He gave them to you—and He wants to show you how to break free from your past so you can grow into your destiny. If He can do it for me, I know He can do it for you.

No matter how trapped you feel—by a stagnant relationship, a dead-end job, debilitating debt, a terrible mistake, or your own fears— you do not have to be stuck there. God has the power and the desire to perform a miracle in your life if you're willing to trust Him with your future. When you do, you'll discover the unique purpose He created just for you.

This book tells my story, but it's also a roadmap designed to lead you closer to the life you long to have. On the pages that follow, you'll learn how to develop a relationship with God, define your vision, quit the excuses that hold you back, attract mentors who can lead you to success, cultivate traits such as integrity and humility, and more. By the last chapter, you will have access to all the tools you need to break out of the traffic jam that's got you stuck so you can hit the open road on a new journey of living the life God designed just for you. Joy, fulfillment, and peace are waiting for you.

Are you ready to make a break for it? Let's get started!

MAKE
A BREAK
FOR IT

1

Dagger to the Heart

There's a divinity that shapes our ends,
Rough-hew them how we will.
William Shakespeare

When I was growing up in the small town of Eufaula, Alabama, thoughts about the future and faith and God were the furthest things from my mind. I did not have a plan for next week, let alone the rest of my life. And church? I just was not interested. I watched people walk into those buildings carrying Bibles and thought they must all be slow readers. Why did it take them so long to finish one book?

My interests were elsewhere, as in motorcycles and girls—not necessarily in that order. Back in the late sixties and early seventies, you could get your motorcycle license at fourteen in Alabama. I saved my money and bought a Harley-Davidson 250 Sprint. It was my first set of wheels, and I was proud of that thing.

I was the only boy in our family, but I had three older sisters—two who were grown and already out of the house and one who was three years older and still at home. My father hadn't wanted a boy and had little to do with me. Much later, I learned there was a name for his behavior: the "alpha male" syndrome. He was jealous and felt threatened by me, afraid I would displace him or somehow take the family's attention away from him. To say my father and I failed to bond would be an understatement.

In my early teens, my father's abusive treatment of my mother left me feeling constantly torn between staying at home to protect her and staying away from home to protect myself. It was a lot of chaos for a kid to endure, but it was my "normal," so I did my best to adapt. The male figures I looked up to and tried to emulate were the older boys in my neighborhood and sometimes their fathers. Because our home was so dysfunctional, I often spent nights with friends or camped out with them on weekends. On one of those weekends, one of the boys brought a big ice chest filled with cans of Budweiser.

"If you want to be a man," he said, "this is what you drink." I was thirteen when I tasted my first beer that night.

The following year, a friend's brother came home from Vietnam and introduced my friends and me to marijuana. No one I knew had even heard of it. I was never addicted or a "stoner," but I did smoke with friends on weekends. When I was fifteen, an older, married woman seduced me into having sex with her. Once that door was opened, I began having sex with other girls. I'm ashamed to say it now, but if they were interested, you could be sure that I was.

Strangely enough, no one seemed to notice or be concerned that I was involved in all of these unhealthy activities. On the outside, I looked like one of the good kids. In fact, I was so good at keeping up appearances I was twice nominated as a "Best Dressed Student." We weren't poor, so I had enough money to buy all the basics. Plus, our family lived in a new home on Lake Eufaula, and we had a boat docked in our backyard. I was athletic and enjoyed sports. When I applied myself, my grades were mostly A's. I also had a lot of friends. As far as anyone could tell, I was a guy who had it all together.

What people couldn't see, however, was the emptiness inside me. I felt aimless. I had no guidance or direction. There wasn't much to do in our small town, so on most weekends I hung out with guys who drank, smoked pot, got into fights, and chased girls. Looking for excitement and adventure, I kept trying new and more reckless things. When a friend threw a cherry bomb through the window of the principal's office, a group of us got suspended. My response was to ride my Harley up the front steps of the school and down a hallway—during class. With the engine noise echoing off the metal lockers, the sound was about ten thousand times louder than I expected. But I was already suspended, so what could they do?

The more I tried stunts like that, however, the less fulfilled I felt. I just had no purpose.

Have you ever felt like that? Or do you feel that way right now? Believe me, I understand what it's like to fool the people around you by pretending everything is great. You also fool yourself, which might work for a while, but it doesn't last. Deep down, you know something isn't right, that something in your life is missing.

All too often, that's how life seems to work, isn't it? Either we're drifting along with no sense of purpose or we're trying to find the answers but getting nowhere. We don't know where we're going, and we don't know why we're here. When we get frustrated and desperate enough, we may try to chart our own course, but we end up in a place that looks nothing like what we had in mind.

That's what happened to me in 1974, the year I was seventeen.

Something's Not Right

My life took two abrupt turns that year. The first was a sudden move to another state. My father started two businesses after he retired from the army: a flooring company and an ice-cream truck operation. They began well but eventually folded. Then he began selling mobile homes and did much better. I didn't know it, but he was in serious debt from the failed businesses, so when the home office for the mobile home company offered him more money if he'd move to Columbus, Georgia, he didn't take long to decide. When I got home from school on a Friday afternoon, my mother was in tears. My father had announced that we were moving from Eufaula to Columbus—the next day. I never even had a chance to say goodbye to my friends. That following Monday, we were in our new town.

The second abrupt turn came on April 28, just a couple of weeks shy of my eighteenth birthday. I'd been cruising the streets of Columbus with a friend in my '69 Camaro late on a Saturday night when I suddenly got an idea. I'd just spotted a young woman standing on a corner. She had long black hair and wore a tight blouse, short black skirt, and high heels.

I turned to my friend. "Danny, you ever been with a prostitute?"

"Nope."

"Me either. Let's try it."

Danny protested, but I ignored him. I swung the car around and pulled up beside the woman.

"What are you doing by yourself on a street corner?" I asked.

"I'm looking for a guy," she said.

"Well, you don't have to look anymore."

As we talked, a man walked up from behind some nearby hedges. He was a couple of inches short of six feet, unshaven, his hair unruly, and had a strong smell of alcohol on his breath. Surprised by his sudden appearance, I briefly wondered if the man was as dangerous as the one he resembled: Lee Harvey Oswald. But I quickly decided that this was "how they do this."

"How much money do y'all have?" the man asked.

Between us, Danny and I had about fifty dollars.

"All right," the man said. "That'll do."

The man and woman got into the backseat of my car and directed me to a dark, run-down, one-story house in a poor neighborhood. The house sat away from the street on the same lot as a pharmacy. It was long and narrow, with an extra room that had been added to the back. We stopped in the gravel parking lot behind the house, where the woman—I didn't know her name—and I got out. We walked to the house's back door while Danny and the man I thought was her pimp sat in the car.

The back room was small, about eight by ten feet. The only furniture was a wardrobe and a bed. A feeble glow emanated from a single, naked bulb in the ceiling. Across the room was another door that led into the rest of the house.

I locked the doorknob and hooked the chain lock on the back door while the woman appeared to lock the door that led into the house, though I later realized she was unlocking it. I wondered what came next. When the woman began taking off her clothes, I did the same. The woman motioned toward the bed. I sat down.

We'd been in the room just a few minutes when she flipped off the light. I couldn't see a thing.

The floor creaked—strange, since the sound didn't seem to come from where the woman had been standing.

I stood up.

Then I smelled an overpowering stench of alcohol—close—the same odor I'd noticed on the pimp's breath.

Alarm bells rang loud and wild in my head. *Something's not right!*

The light suddenly switched back on. I was initially blinded, but then I saw that the pimp was in the room—and he was holding a twelve-inch butcher knife.

The man smiled, but it wasn't friendly.

"Now," he said, "you're gonna die!"

Before I could react, he thrust the knife hard at my chest. I winced and felt a hot surge through my body. I looked down and saw the knife blade plunged completely inside me, the handle stopped against my chest. The blade had missed my heart by a quarter inch.

The woman screamed and kept screaming.

The pimp yanked out the knife and thrust it at me again. The blow was aimed at my head, but I jerked back. This time the blade entered my neck and came out the other side. It severed my jugular vein. Though I didn't know it at the time, when the jugular is completely cut, most people bleed out in less than four minutes.

Adrenaline shot through me. *I've got to fight my way out of here!*

As my attacker jerked the knife out a second time, I punched with my left hand, hitting him in the upper chest and throat. He started to fall. With my right arm, I instinctively hooked the man's leg and pulled. His head hit the floor with a loud thud.

I saw my chance. I leapt over his body, which blocked my way to the back door and freedom. But he wasn't finished with me yet. As I jumped, he stabbed a third time. This time the blade sliced into my liver.

I continued my forward motion until I reached the door. I turned the handle, but it didn't give. *I'd locked it!* I was running out of time. The pimp was getting up from the floor, and I was too panicked to unlock the door and remove the chain lock.

Knowing I didn't have a second to spare, my adrenaline pumping, I stepped back, lowered my shoulder, and rammed the door with all the strength I could find. It broke from its hinges and fell down flat.

Half running, half stumbling, I raced toward the Camaro, where a horrified Danny sat in the driver's seat. Danny later told me he'd heard the loud noise and banging sounds from inside the room and didn't know what to think or do. As he squinted, trying to see in the darkness, the door suddenly broke loose and there I stood, naked and covered in blood, the lone light swinging from the ceiling behind me. He said it looked like something from a horror movie.

I made it to the car and stumbled against the hood, yelling, "Get out of here!" I ran across the street and into a parking lot next to a deserted theater, where I wrapped my arms around a metal light pole. Slowly, my strength fading, I slid to the ground, smearing the light pole with blood.

I stared up at the stars, gasping for breath, choking on my own blood. My heart was pounding so hard it felt like it would bust out of my chest. I'd suffered three devastating wounds. Any one of them was enough to kill me, and I had no doubt I was dying. A friend had died from a single ice pick wound to the stomach. I couldn't imagine I'd survive this.

Of all the things a dying young man might think of in his final moments, a brief conversation with someone I barely knew is not what I would have expected. But as I clung to what was left of my life, one sentence from that conversation entered my mind, clearly and calmly. They were words I'd heard just two weeks before.

I'd been at home when there was a knock at the door and I'd answered it. There stood a slim fellow in glasses, maybe seventeen years old.

"B-B-Bill," the visitor stammered, "everything you're looking for can be found in Jesus."

I stared at him without speaking.

"I gotta go," he said nervously and ran away.

I hadn't known what to make of it. Only later did I learn that God had prompted this young man to come to my door and share his faith. He'd been in a church meeting when the speaker challenged the young people to witness to the most "lost" person they knew. Though he didn't know me well, this boy felt he had to talk to me. He wondered if anyone had ever told me about Jesus.

At the time, I just shook my head and tried to forget about it. But that boy messed me up. Have you ever had a song stuck in your head? That's what it was like for me. Every day, whenever it was quiet, his words kept replaying in my mind: *Everything you're looking for can be found in Jesus.*

As I clung to the light pole and anticipated the end of my life, the words from that strange encounter came back to me again.

I wasn't a churchgoing guy. I didn't read the Bible, and I'd never prayed in my life. But I decided it was now or never. "Jesus," I cried out as I choked on my own blood, "help me. Save me. Please forgive me of my sins. Help me, God. Please save me."

I heard Danny trying to start the Camaro. Tires squealed and the roar of the engine grew louder until he skidded to a stop beside me. I somehow managed to get to the car and dived in the passenger seat. "Get me to a hospital!" I shouted.

Danny raced to the Columbus Medical Center, which fortunately for me was only half a block away. At the emergency room entrance, I used the last bit of adrenaline I had left to walk up to an orderly who'd stepped outside for a cigarette break. He had his back turned and didn't see me coming. I wrapped my arms around him and choked out, "I need some help, buddy."

The orderly grabbed me, ran inside, threw me onto a gurney, and rushed me inside the emergency room, leaving behind a trail of blood. Three doctors immediately came in. One was Philip Brewer, a renowned cardiothoracic vascular surgeon who happened to have stayed past the end of his shift that day. Another was Larry Brightwell, a trauma specialist who'd served in the Army Medical Corps in Vietnam. The third was Robert Lightenor, an emergency room physician.

One of the doctors examined my throat. "Get the district attorney up here," he said. "This boy's been stabbed to death. His jugular vein's completely cut. He's not dead yet, but he will be before the DA gets here."

I was still conscious and heard everything he'd said. I knew my time was almost up.

Doug Pullen, assistant district attorney, happened to be riding for the first time with a police officer that night. He showed up minutes later. He said it was easy to find the right room; he just followed the trail of blood. "It looked," he said later, "like someone had taken a bucket of red paint and poured it down the hallway." After being told I was about to die, Pullen asked me a few questions about what happened.

A doctor soon interrupted. "I have to start surgery now." Then the anesthesia kicked in and I was out.

Second Life

I regained consciousness eleven hours later. I didn't have the strength to move, but I could turn my head enough to take in my surroundings. I was in a hospital bed hooked up to all kinds of machines. Through the open door, I could see policemen standing in the hallway outside my room and nurses walking by. Then memories from the night before came flooding back. It hadn't been a dream—I was supposed to be dead! But this didn't look like heaven or hell. It was the hospital. Somehow, I was alive. As I replayed the events that had led me here, I remembered. *You prayed and asked God to come into your life and save you.*

It was the only possible explanation for the fact that I was still alive. I was deeply humbled. I felt I didn't deserve to be alive. I also felt that I was too sinful and unworthy to have any favor or mercy from God. I always thought He loved only the good people. I prayed again: "God, thank You for what You did. Thank You for helping me. But You don't know what You got last night. You got somebody You can't use or do anything with. If You don't ever want to have anything to do with me or hear from me again, I understand. I won't bother You anymore."

The strangest feeling came over me in that moment. I felt both a peace in my heart and a sense of God's loving amusement, almost as if He were chuckling at my naiveté.

Then, to my surprise, I sensed a response to my prayer.

Bill, just do what I tell you to do from now on. Let Me do the rest.

It was a turning point, the beginning of my second life.

A few days into my recovery, I suddenly had the most intense hunger for the Bible. I wasn't even a reader of regular books, but once I found a Gideon Bible in the hospital nightstand, it was like the greatest gift I'd ever received. In another sign of God's surprising interest in me, a nurse who noticed my craving for the Bible asked me what I was reading one day.

"Spasms," I said.

"Spasms?" she asked.

We eventually figured out that what I thought was "spasms" was actually the book of Psalms. When it came to spiritual matters, I was totally clueless.

Over the next few days, she started to come in thirty minutes early for her shift so she could spend time reading and explaining the Bible to me. When she got to the story about Jesus walking on water, I protested.

"Hold on," I said. "What do you mean, He walked on water? Nobody walks on water."

"He saved *you*, didn't He?" she said.

I decided she had a point. "Read on."

The more I learned about the Bible, the hungrier I was to learn more about God. It was the most amazing thing. The doctors were amazed too—not so much at my spiritual transformation, but because I was still breathing. The night of the attack, a doctor told the assistant district attorney, Doug Pullen, that I wouldn't make it until morning. In the morning, doctors said I was still alive, but it was unlikely I would survive. The next morning, Pullen was told that I might live, but if I did, I would have no mental capacity. I'd been without oxygen for too long.

Instead, though I'd lost eight pints of blood and required over one hundred stitches, I made a complete recovery. I am one of a handful of people in the world who have survived a severed jugular vein.

Six months after I was stabbed, the pimp was arrested, charged with aggravated assault, and sentenced to ten years in prison. His plan, forced on his wife, had been to lure an unsuspecting teen to the house. While in the car with Danny, he'd said he was going to take a walk to have a cigarette. Instead, he moved quickly to the front of the house, grabbed a butcher knife as he passed through the kitchen, and waited for the signal from his wife. When the light went out, he slipped into the room through the unlocked door, intending to kill me and steal my money. But the would-be murderers didn't count on my left hook, much less my deathbed prayer and miraculous recovery.

"The only reason I can give you for Bill Purvis being alive right now is that God had a purpose for him," Doug Pullen later said in an interview recorded for our church. "He wanted him to fulfill that purpose. Even the doctors will tell you that this is one they can chalk up to God, not to anything they did."

You Don't Have to Wait

I should have died that night in Columbus, but God healed me—physically and spiritually—and gave me another chance. Everything I have and cherish today—my wife, my children and grandchildren, my friends, my church, my home—is the result of what God did for me beginning that night. The only explanation for my continued existence is that God spared my life so He could show me His amazing grace. There is a beautiful passage from the Psalms that captures my story and always reminds me of that miracle when I read it:

> He brought me up out of the pit of destruction, out of the
>   miry clay,
> And He set my feet upon a rock making my footsteps firm.
> He put a new song in my mouth, a song of praise to
>   our God;
> Many will see and fear
> And will trust in the LORD. (Psalm 40:2–3)

It took a violent attack and a miraculous recovery for me to realize that God holds my destiny in His hands. But you don't have to be like me. You don't have to wait until you're staring death in the face to discover the path to your purpose.

God loves you, and He really does have a unique and amazing plan for you, too. If you're willing to join me on this adventure, I want to help you break through the obstacles you face—outside of you and within you—to uncover the destiny God imagined for you before you were born. I can't tell you what your purpose is, but I can promise you that it's far more exciting and fulfilling than anything you've experienced in life so far.

Let's continue the journey together.

Insights for Inspiration

- When something is missing from your life, you may be able to fool others, but you can't fool yourself.

- If you're on the wrong track and traveling away from your purpose, you're headed for more frustration and more trouble.

- God loves you and has a unique plan and purpose for your life.

Verse to Review

"And looking at them Jesus said to them, 'With people this is impossible, but with God all things are possible'" (Matthew 19:26).

Getting Personal

- Overall, how would you describe your life so far—that you have had a strong sense of purpose, that you have had little or no sense of purpose, or that your sense of purpose comes and goes in different seasons of life? Which best describes your life right now?

- How have you handled the times when you felt little or no sense of purpose? What was the result?

- Do you have a sense of what God's destiny for you might be? If so, describe where you think God may be leading you. If not, what is it you most hope God might change in your life as you begin this journey of discovering your purpose?

2

Uniquely You

*It takes courage to grow up and
become who you really are.*
E. E. Cummings

L et's talk about love.
When I say love, I don't mean flowers and fancy dinners and
romance. And I also don't mean times when you say you "love" that
black evening gown or pineapple on your pizza or the Dallas Cowboys.
No, what I want to talk about is the deep, overflowing kind of love that
is always ready to sacrifice everything. It's the unconditional love that
lasts forever.

Have you experienced that kind of love? Most people encounter it
for the first time in their families as they grow up. "A mother's love" is
a catchphrase for a reason—moms are known for their fierce devotion
to their children. One of the most powerful stories I know that demonstrates this kind of love happened in Germany during World War II.

A young Jewish family among the millions forced to perform hard
labor in concentration camps were together in one camp but separated
from each other every morning to perform their duties. On his return
to the barracks each evening, the family's father, Solomon, frantically
scanned faces searching for his wife and two sons, David and Jacob.
He never knew when a guard might decide to send one of them to the

gas chamber. He especially feared for David, his youngest, who was handicapped.

One night, Solomon's worst fears were realized. When he looked through the crowd in the barracks, he couldn't find his family. When he finally found his oldest son, the boy was hunched over and weeping.

"Jacob," Solomon said, "tell me it isn't so. Did they take David today?"

"Yes, Papa," Jacob said. "Today they came to take David. They said he could no longer do his work."

"But Mama, where is Mama? She is still strong. Surely they didn't take Mama, too?"

"Papa, Papa," he said, "When they came to take David, he was afraid and he cried. So Mama said to David, 'Don't cry, David, I will go with you and hold you close.' So Mama went with him to the ovens so he wouldn't be afraid."[1]

This is the kind of sacrificial and unconditional love that so many mothers understand. There isn't anything they wouldn't do for the sake of their children.

That's how my mom loved me. She was always there for me. She taught me how to read, ride a bike, throw and catch a ball, fish, and shoot a gun. She was a big encourager who saw the best in everybody. She believed that if everyone just had a fair chance, they would make it in life. She supported and inspired me in so many ways as I grew up.

As I've already mentioned, this was not the case with my father. He enjoyed the attention of women, but having another male in the house was a different story. When I was young, my older sister, Sonja, sometimes took me with her when she went out of the house, even on her dates. She feared our father might hurt me. Once when I was old enough to play Little League baseball, my father and I stopped at a gas station, where we ran into my baseball coach.

"Bill really puts his heart into the game," the coach told my dad. "I sure appreciate having him on the team." Without saying a word, my dad drove off and left that coach standing there. He didn't want to hear anyone bragging about me.

We rarely celebrated Christmas or birthdays—not because my father didn't believe in such things, but because he was cheap. In later years, after I was an adult, my wife and children each gave my father unique and nice gifts. He responded with gifts of his own, such as toys for his grandchildren. But when it came time for me to open a gift from my father, my family braced themselves. His gifts to me always seemed to have an insult attached. One year he said, "Hey, I never got you a car when you were sixteen—here you go." My present was a Matchbox car. Another year he said, "I didn't give you a pair of shoes when you were five, so maybe you can use these." My gift was a tiny pair of tennis shoes he'd picked up at a flea market. My family was angered by his behavior, but for me it was just "normal."

By the time my father was an old man, he and I had no relationship. When his health declined, I decided to call him every two weeks as a last attempt at making some kind of connection with him. It didn't happen. I kept calling in hopes of getting the breakthrough or the blessing I'd wanted my whole life, but I always ended the conversations wishing I'd never reached out. I did this for two years until he started down the path of insulting my sons, just as he'd always insulted me. That was the day he crossed the line. Something inside me finally accepted the sad reality of who my father was.

My mother had passed away a few years before, after a battle with cancer. Before she died, she handed me a thirteen-page, handwritten letter sealed in an envelope. "If your father ever gets really mean," she said, "you open this letter."

I didn't give it a lot of thought the day she gave me the letter. My father was mean enough already, so I wasn't sure what "really mean" would look like. I put the envelope away and forgot about it. But after my mother's death and my father's subsequent remarriage, sure enough, he seemed to get even meaner. When I came across that letter one day at home, I pondered what I should do. *Do I really want to know what is inside? What if it only deepens the rejection I feel?* Finally, I opened it.

Bill, I just want you to know that I wanted you. You were always wanted. Your father never knew how to love a boy. I wanted a boy, thinking that would be what he wanted. I assumed every man wanted a son. After you were born, I began to see that he could not have another male in the house. It was nothing you ever did that caused the gap in your relationship. The issues were his. If you can overlook his feelings toward you and not wonder what you ever did, you can succeed. I've always loved you and have always been proud of you.

Reading that letter was like finding the missing piece of my past. It made so much sense to me. The words of songwriter Johnny Nash described exactly how I felt: "I can see clearly now." I was flooded with a peace I'd never known—a peace that was followed by a sense of freedom to move on and gently shut the door on the painful relationship with my father.

My father never graduated from high school. His personal regret over that unfinished achievement caused him to belittle people who had an education or wanted one. My mother, on the other hand, believed that education opened doors. While I was building a marriage, raising my family, and pastoring a church, I'd started work on a master's degree in divinity. However, given all the responsibilities I was juggling, at one point I considered postponing my studies. In a conversation with my mother before she died, she pleaded with me. "Bill, I wish you'd finish your master's," she said. My education and personal growth were so important to her.

My mother lost her battle with cancer just a few days after Princess Diana of Wales died in Paris on August 31, 1997. Before the week was over, Mother Teresa of Calcutta, India, had also died. I've always felt the world lost three great women that week.

Just over a year later, I stood on a platform and received my first master's degree. When the graduates left the stage, we walked into a long hallway that ended in a room where we were to meet and celebrate with our families. While in the hallway, I slipped out of line and into a little room filled with mops and other cleaning equipment. I closed the door so no one around could see me, but I knew someone was watching from above. I raised that diploma high, looked up, and said, "I did this for you, Mom."

My mother was a caring, open, honest person. What you saw was what you got. I believe I inherited some of those qualities from her. As I talked with my father on the phone one day, near the end of his life, he remarked on how much I was like my mother. Except to him, that was a fault. "You act just like your mother," he said.

Near the end of our conversation, I put my feelings on the line. "All I ever wanted in my life was for my father to say, 'I love you.'"

"I would never say that," was his response. That was our last discussion. He died less than a year later.

I know I'm not the only person who's had a hunger for acceptance and love from someone close, yet been rejected. Maybe you've had the same experience with one or both of your parents. Maybe it was a spouse who cheated on you or a friend or sibling who betrayed you. I don't know your story, but I understand that when love is withdrawn or never offered, it hurts all the way down to the core of your soul. It feels like an aching hole that will never be filled and never stop hurting.

But you know what? There is someone who can fill that hole. Someone with enough love to fill the earth's oceans and still never run dry. Someone who cares about you with a fierce and powerful love.

That someone is God.

Creating Something Special

As a small child, I'd been to church a few times with my mother and tried to sing along with the rest of the congregation. As a teenager, I watched people go to church on Sundays and figured they were trying to be good people. I didn't look down on them or have anything against them. It just wasn't me. Unless there was a pretty girl involved, I saw no reason to go.

I did believe in God. It made sense to me that someone had created this world and everything in it. I just didn't see that it had much to do with me or my life. Most of my friends felt the same way. When it came to spiritual matters, we were ignorant.

One day when I was a teenager, I was driving to Alabama with two buddies, Greg and Ken. At one point, Greg turned to us and said, "My dad got saved last week."

I was practically raised on Lake Eufaula. To me, getting saved meant someone had fallen into the water and nearly drowned. "That's cool," I said. "I'm glad to hear it. He almost died?"

"No, Bill," Greg said, "he didn't fall out of a boat. He got saved."

"What is saved?" I asked.

"He got his sins forgiven."

"How?"

"He got saved."

"Bill, you've never been saved," Ken broke in, "so you wouldn't understand."

"Well," I said, "help me understand!"

The problem was that my friends didn't know any more about being saved than I did.

"You have to go to church," Ken said. "And you have to shake the preacher's hand."

I shook my head. "Nah, that don't work," I said. "Last week I was riding my motorcycle in the parking lot at Parkview Baptist Church.

The pastor flagged me down and asked me to help him put an air conditioner in his office window. So I did, and when we were done he shook my hand and thanked me. But I'm no different."

"No, no," Ken said. "You got to walk down the center aisle of the church first."

"We did! We walked right down the center on the way to his office."

That stumped my friends for a minute. But then Ken had the answer.

"Was the music playing?" he asked.

"No," I said. "It was a Friday afternoon. There wasn't any music."

"That's why you weren't saved!" Ken said. "There has to be music playing."

Greg added his agreement. "Yeah, that's how you get saved, Bill," he said.

"I don't think either of you know what you're talking about," I said. It was the blind leading the blind.

Perhaps you can relate. It could be that until recently you've never shown much interest in God or spiritual matters. Or it could be that what you think you know about God isn't much more accurate than what my friends tried to tell me. Whatever the case, I urge you to check Him out for yourself and discover the real truth, because not knowing is missing out on why we were created in the first place.

My indifferent attitude about God continued for the rest of my teen years—all the way up to that wild night in Columbus. It took a desperate prayer and a miraculous recovery from what should have been a fatal stabbing for me to see what I could have seen all along: *God really loves me.* And I don't mean the way you might love your grandmother's apple pie. I'm talking about the kind of love that is complete, sacrificial, and unconditional. The kind of love a mother in a concentration camp has for her doomed child.

God loves you that way too. The evidence runs all throughout the Bible from beginning to end. In the first book of the Bible, we read,

"God created human beings in his own image" (Gen. 1:27 NLT). What does that tell you? It tells me that God had something very specific in mind when He made men and women. This was not a last-minute recipe He threw together, hoping it might turn out okay. Far from it. God patterned us after Himself. I don't think being made in God's image means a physical resemblance, but that we have the potential to take on the same qualities of character God Himself possesses: love, compassion, patience, wisdom, and many more. That indicates that God cares a great deal about His creation.

Here is how the psalmist describes the care God demonstrated in creating us:

> For You formed my inward parts;
> You wove me in my mother's womb.
> I will give thanks to You, for I am fearfully and
>   wonderfully made;
> Wonderful are Your works,
> And my soul knows it very well. (Psalm 139:13–14)

Let those words soak in for a minute—they're just as true of you as they were of the psalmist. God formed you. You are wonderfully made. His work is wonderful. Doesn't it sound like God values and appreciates what He's done with you? Doesn't it seem like He must view you as something special?

Of course, the real proof of God's love for us came about two thousand years ago when God saw how many mistakes we were making on this earth. He knew we needed help, someone who could step in and accept responsibility for those mistakes. So He made the biggest sacrifice a parent can make. He sent His only Son, Jesus, to die a terrible death on our behalf so that we could know Him forever—so we could be saved: "For God so loved the world, that He gave His only begotten Son, that whoever believes in Him shall not perish, but have eternal life" (John 3:16).

I know some people view God as a harsh judge sitting up high somewhere, just waiting to condemn the guilty for everything they've done wrong. They see the Bible as a book of laws or rules and feel weighed down by the responsibility and God's expectations. I think people who have a hard time in life or people who grow up with a parent like my father are even more likely to see God this way. All I can say is that from my experience and perspective, it's just not true—God is not a tyrant in the sky who delights in zapping people when they mess up.

When I was in that Columbus hospital and began reading the Bible for the first time, I felt like I was reading a letter from the loving father I'd never known. I didn't see God as a judge waiting to administer punishment with a bullwhip but as a parent with tears of compassion in His eyes. When I read in the Old Testament about His judgment of people who had disobeyed and mocked Him, I felt reassured that He was just and in control. When I read about Jesus, I better understood God's mind and heart—and the love He has for me and each one of His children.

God's love is like the love I get from my grandkids. When I walk in the door and they're in the house, I don't have to bring a present or do anything special to get their affection. As soon as they see me, they shout, "Big Daddy's here!" and come running. They want me to sit down with them so they can show me the pictures they've drawn or tell me what they've been doing. Their love for me is pure, innocent, and powerful.

That's what God's love feels like to me. And His love is just as strong for you as it is for me. As I write this, one of my daughters-in-law is expecting a baby girl. I don't yet know exactly what she'll look like, but I love that baby already. She is part of our family. In a similar way, God loved you before you even knew Him or came into this world. He'll also love you long after you leave your earthly life.

When the Bible says God so loved the world, *so loved* means from vanishing point to vanishing point—as far to the horizon as you can see.

People will let you down. Some will love you only if you do or give them what they want. Some won't love you no matter what you do. But God's love for you never ceases—it keeps flowing and flowing, forever.

Like me, my sister Sonja went through life feeling unloved by our father. It was a love she yearned for but never experienced—her missing ingredient. She did come to know God, however. When I was recovering after the stabbing, I stayed with Sonja and her husband, Rick, in Demopolis, Alabama, for a few months. They had recently become followers of Christ, and their newfound faith, nightly Bible reading, and prayers were exactly what I needed. Even so, because of our age difference and the dysfunction of our family, she and I rarely connected in the years that followed.

Not long ago, with my wife's encouragement, I called Sonja and invited her to stay with us for a few days. We talked about many things, including the love of God. She confessed that she'd never known our father's love herself. When she was twelve, my father sent her away to live with my mother's sister.

These days, Sonja and I talk on the phone almost every week. She says God has used our relationship to show her that despite her painful, lonely past, God has brought healing. "The hole in my heart all of these years from my childhood, and from never feeling that I was wanted or belonged, has been filled," she says. "God used my baby brother to teach me how much God loves me and how I am accepted by Him."

I want that hole to be filled for you, too. When you allow God's love to pour into you, you lay a foundation that enables you to pursue your true purpose. It is only when this foundation is set that you can begin living a new life of freedom and peace.

A Masterpiece in Waiting

One way to better understand just how much God loves you is to consider how much you love your own unique creations. I want you to really think about this. When have you put your whole heart and soul into creating something? It might have been a painting, a novel, a quilt, a wedding dress. Maybe it was a 1960s sports car you rebuilt from old parts. Perhaps it was a gourmet dinner for friends, a beautiful garden, or even a new home. It might have taken you weeks or months to make it, possibly even years.

You don't put that much effort into a project on a whim. It's something you plan for and invest time in for a purpose. It's not a copy of someone else's labors but something personal, your very best work, rare and irreplaceable. If it's a painting, you wouldn't leave that canvas out in the rain and allow it to be ruined, would you? And you wouldn't hide it in the attic where no one could see it—not unless you thought it was a pretty terrible painting. If it's something you're proud of, something special you want people to appreciate, you'll have a plan for making it happen.

Imagine, then, how God must feel about you. It just makes sense that if His love for you is so great—from vanishing point to vanishing point—He isn't going to let you collect dust in the attic. He has a plan and purpose for your life—it's what you were made for. If you refuse to believe in God's abundant love and distinct plans for you, you'll lack the security and confidence of knowing that your identity and self-worth come from your favored position as a child of God. Without that confidence, you'll spend your limited time and energy battling self-defeating obstacles rather than pursuing your destiny. God has plans for you, and those plans take root when you accept the gift of God's love and purpose for you.

Through the prophet Jeremiah, God once said to His people, "For I know the plans that I have for you,' declares the LORD, 'plans for welfare and not for calamity to give you a future and a hope'" (Jer. 29:11). That captures what God has in store for you—a future and a hope.

If it's still hard for you to believe God really does have a plan for you, think about it this way. God is the artist who created you, and His creations are never haphazard or second rate. When great sculptors like Donatello, Michelangelo, and Rodin approached a block of marble, they didn't just randomly begin to whack away chunks of stone. They had a plan—a vision of what they wanted to create. Then they used specialized chisels and files to patiently chip away the rough exterior until what was left was a work of rare beauty.

God's works of art are not sculpted out of stone but out of human lives. You and I are His masterpieces. You may not feel much like a beautiful work of art. In fact, maybe with the way your life has been going, you feel more like an ugly lump of clay. But in the loving hands of a master artist, every lump of clay can be transformed into something unique, beautiful, and useful.

Remember the prophet Jeremiah? God delivered this message to him one day:

> The word which came to Jeremiah from the LORD saying, "Arise and go down to the potter's house, and there I will announce My words to you." Then I went down to the potter's house, and there he was, making something on the wheel. But the vessel that he was making of clay was spoiled in the hand of the potter; so he remade it into another vessel, as it pleased the potter to make.
>
> Then the word of the LORD came to me saying, "Can I not, O house of Israel, deal with you as this potter does?" declares the LORD. "Behold, like the clay in the potter's hand, so are you in My hand, O house of Israel." (Jeremiah 18:1–6)

This is exactly what God wants to do with you. You may look at yourself and see only a lump of clay, but God has a specific plan for you. He sees the unique masterpiece just waiting to take shape and understands precisely what needs to happen to bring it about.

So what prevents us from realizing this God-designed destiny? All too often, it's us. *We* are the roadblock sitting in the way of the plan. Because we don't believe God loves us or don't trust that He created us in a unique way to fulfill His specific plan, we veer off course. We try to push and promote ourselves into a place of significance, or we give up and allow ourselves to settle for less than our destiny. I'll say it again: We will never discover the joy and fulfillment God desires to give us until we believe in our hearts that God loves us and that He designed us specifically for His unique purpose.

Why do we doubt? Maybe we feel that God is too busy, that we're not a priority, or that He can't possibly love us when there are literally billions of other people in the world to care for. Yet the Bible tells us we are "precious" in His sight and "honored" (Isa. 43:4) and that He knows the number and name of every star (Ps. 147:4). Doesn't a God who can create the universe and keep track of every star have the ability to love us personally?

Won't you take the risk to trust the God who made you and loves you so much? Here's a simple prayer to get you started: "God, You know where I am. I know if I draw close to You, You'll navigate my life. You'll put me in the right place at the right time with the right people. I trust You with my life and my future." God's purposes for you may or may not include fame and fortune. Perhaps your destiny is hidden within a life of quiet service. But you can be sure that God's unique plan for you will be meaningful, exciting, and rewarding to *you*.

You and I may already have a plan for our lives, but I promise you, if God's not behind it, the plan is too small. He sees the big picture and knows exactly what we need and where we will be most useful and fulfilled. So how do we get out of the way so we can discover that destiny? How do we overcome our resistance to change so we can grow into the people God wants us to be?

That is precisely what we'll be talking about next.

Insights for Inspiration

- God's love for us is complete, sacrificial, and unconditional.
- God doesn't love us *if* we change. He has loved us, imperfections and all, from the beginning.
- We are like lumps of clay waiting to be shaped into masterpieces.

Verse to Review

"Trust in the LORD with all your heart and do not lean on your own understanding" (Proverbs 3:5).

Getting Personal

- Who has loved you unconditionally? How did you know or discover that this person loved you no matter what?
- On a scale of one to ten (one being low, ten being high), how strong is your belief that God loves you unconditionally? Is the number the highest it's ever been, the lowest, or somewhere in between? Why?
- Briefly identify one or two people you love unconditionally. How would you describe your hopes for them?
- If you could give the people you love a sense of purpose and a meaningful life, would you do it? What, if anything, keeps you from believing God desires to do the same for you?

---- 3 ----

Breaking Free

Liberty is always dangerous, but it
is the safest thing we have.
Harry Emerson Fosdick

When was the last time you visited the ocean? Did you watch the waves roll in and smell the saltwater? Did you take off your shoes to put your feet in the sand? If you looked down at all, you might have seen a crab, or at least the remains of the hard outer shell that protects a crab. On some beaches, there are seasons when dozens of empty crab shells wash up along the shore and you might think there's been an ecological disaster that killed them off. But an empty crab shell isn't necessarily the carcass of a dead crab. In fact, it is more likely to be evidence of a healthy and growing crab.

Every time a crab grows, it has to discard its old shell. It cracks open its exterior shell, tears it away, and then grows a new one—a process known as molting. Molting occurs repeatedly throughout the life of a crab until it finally stops growing. And it's not a painless process. During molting, the crab's muscle attachments are torn away from the old shell, which makes it difficult for the crab to move. When the crab finally does crawl out of its shell, the soft and unprotected crustacean is vulnerable to predators until its new shell is fully formed.

The risk and hassle might seem hardly worth the trouble. So why does the crab risk changing shells? *Because when it stops growing, it soon stops living.* The same hard shell that protects the crab eventually prohibits its continued growth. A growing crab will die if it does not break out of its restrictive shell. So the crab has to make a choice: endure short-term pain or cease to exist.

When it comes to growth, you and I have a lot in common with the crab. We have been designed to grow throughout our lives. Our physical growth begins at conception and continues into early adulthood. The intellectual, emotional, relational, and spiritual areas of our lives are healthiest when they are growing—and if we're willing to keep changing, we continue growing for the rest of our lives, which is precisely what God designed us for. I love how author C. S. Lewis describes God's vision for us:

> No possible degree of holiness or heroism which has ever been recorded of the greatest saints is beyond what He is determined to produce in every one of us in the end. The job will not be completed in this life: but He means to get us as far as possible before death.[1]

In other words, God has some pretty big growth plans for us, and we may as well get used to the process now because we're going to spend eternity growing!

There's no way around it. In order to discover our destiny, we have to follow God's plan for change and growth.

Are You a Crab or a Chameleon?

Because growth requires change and change is uncomfortable or even frightening for many of us, it's important to understand how we feel about change and how we tend to respond to it. In my three decades as a pastor and Christian leader, I've discovered that people tend to have one of two responses when it comes to the legitimate risks associated with change—they respond like crabs or chameleons. While change is a lifestyle for the crab, change avoidance is the lifestyle for the chameleon. Here are a few characteristics of both.

CRABS	CHAMELEONS
Seek growth and are willing to risk vulnerability and discomfort to achieve it.	Seek security and are willing to adapt outwardly to get it.
Want to make progress so they can break out of whatever keeps them from growing.	Want to keep things the same so they can avoid having to deal with whatever keeps them from growing.
Are willing to persevere through hardships, including criticism or rejection, in pursuit of growth.	Are unwilling to pursue growth if there is a risk of losing acceptance through criticism or rejection.
Choose a hard path in the short term and reap the rewards of growth in the long term.	Choose an easy path in the short term and end up paying the price of being stuck and stagnant in the long term.

Which creature do you relate to most, the chameleon or the crab? Can you think of times you've chosen to be a chameleon by blending in to life as it is rather than breaking free like a crab into a better, larger life? Are you stuck in a pattern of blending in right now? If so, you're far from alone.

At some point in life, most of us find ways to protect ourselves by blending in. In fact, from the time we're children, we learn that people like us best when we look like, think like, talk like, walk like, and act like them. Every culture develops its own unwritten rules about what it means to fit in and to be liked. As a result, we feel pressure to conform to whatever our culture considers "acceptable" at the time.

You've probably seen this happen in the workplace. Your team is discussing a job applicant and everyone thinks the potential hire is wonderful—everyone except you. Something inside you is raising a red flag about his character. The needle on your instinct meter begins to move, but you're new on the team or have less authority, so you decline to speak up. You go along—protect yourself by blending in—because you don't want to risk rejection or disapproval. A few months later, you feel sick inside when you hear that the new hire has destroyed relationships, embezzled from the organization, and hurt its good reputation. Why didn't you speak up? Because doing so would have forced you out of your comfort zone, the place where you feel safe from judgment and ridicule. However, you missed an opportunity to push beyond self-protective behaviors for the greater good of your workplace. In the process, you also lost out on a growth opportunity that could have helped you to develop greater confidence and strength of character.

Often we allow cultural pressures and the expectations of others to influence our personal growth and choices much more than we realize. For example, a man or woman might like to be a stay-at-home parent but is afraid to resign, knowing friends will look down on this decision not to "work" outside the home. Or a young man wants to go to school to become a teacher but his family admires only high-paying careers in such fields as engineering, law, and medicine. He keeps his real passion hidden because risking disapproval is too painful. What he wants and feels called to do is overruled by a stronger desire to fit in and live up to his family's expectations. As a result, the young man stops growing and, for a time at least, is derailed from pursuing his purpose.

This pressure to conform—to stay safe by blending in—even happens to us in church. We feel pressure to dress the same, look the same, talk the same, think the same, smile the same, and worship the same as the people sitting around us. Doubts about your faith? Problems with your marriage? Dreams of a different life? Too often, the church fails to be a safe place to step out from the shadows and talk about such things.

That's why it's easier to look the part (like a chameleon) rather than tear off the façade and acknowledge the naked truth (like a crab). The result is that we stunt our growth and only become better actors instead of better Christians.

I'm not advocating change simply for the sake of change. That's no more effective than rearranging the furniture in a house that desperately needs renovations. If you want to discover your purpose, change that leads to growth is the kind of change you want. You can start by identifying the areas in your life where you feel stuck. What do you wish was different in those areas of your life? Now think about the changes you need to make, not so much as losses or hardships but simply as an exchange—just like the crab exchanges an old shell for a new one. My friend Diane Debardeleben says it this way: "You have to decide between what you want now and what you want most." If you can learn to see change as exchange—as trading up for something better—you can leverage your faith against your fears. And you'll know you're on the right track if you're changing in a way that brings you closer to God and develops your faith.

You're probably wondering if there is a way to escape the chameleon trap and grow into your purpose. Of course there is! As you might expect, it was designed by God. It begins when you allow God to renew your mind, and it continues when you commit to saying yes to whatever God asks you to do.

Allow God to Renew Your Mind

God wants to bring about lasting change in each of us but without making us carbon copies of everyone else or forcing us to live up to other people's expectations of who we should be. Instead, God invites us to grow first in our relationship with Him. That loving relationship is what enables us to shed whatever is holding us back and to welcome whatever will lead us into a more fulfilling future. It's a growth process that starts when we're born into God's family. Here's how the apostle Paul describes it:

> Do not be *conformed* to this world, but be *transformed* by the renewing of your mind, so that you may prove what the will of God is, so that which is good and acceptable and perfect. (Romans 12:2, emphasis added)

In other words, if you want to embrace what God has designed specifically for you, you have to reject the temptation to conform to the world's expectations. To keep yourself from conforming, you have to be "transformed by the renewing of your mind." The original Greek word translated "transformed" is *metamorphousthe*, from which we get the English word *metamorphosis*. In this case, we're not talking about a onetime change but a lifelong process of ongoing change. You have to keep changing, because when you stop changing you tend to start conforming. But when your fear of conforming is greater than your fear of change, you are well on your way to realizing your dreams.

This renewal of the mind is God's way of bringing about the right kind of change. It doesn't happen overnight, but it does happen. When we spend time talking with God, worshiping Him, and meditating on His words in the Bible, our minds begin to change. We find that instead of resisting the changes God wants us to make, we are increasingly open to where He wants to lead us. We actually begin to think and see things from God's perspective, which is part of what it means to "have the mind of Christ" (1 Cor. 2:16 NIV).

How does this happen? Let's revisit the crab for a moment. Do you know how the crab begins the process of breaking out of its old shell? It rapidly absorbs a lot of water. When its tissues swell with fluid, the old shell splits open, which enables the crab to begin breaking free of it. That's something like what happens when you soak yourself in Scripture. When you absorb the Word of God on a regular basis and meditate on it, it begins to cleanse your mind and heart, making it easier to discard old habits of thought and behavior. And if you'll let Him, God will use any discomfort you may experience in the change process to motivate and equip you. In fact, the promise of Scripture is that "God is working in you, giving you the desire and the power to do what pleases him" (Phil. 2:13 NLT). Did you catch that? When your mind is aligned with the mind of God, you *can* change because you have both the desire and the power to do so.

People sometimes ask whether it's God or us who does the changing. The answer is *both*! God gives us the desire and power to change, but we have to walk by faith as we do our part, too. For example, every December my wife and I write out several areas in which we want to experience growth in the year to come. We list our spiritual, physical, intellectual, financial, and relational goals, and we write out exactly what we intend to do to pursue growth in those areas. Then we monitor our progress in each area once a month. Small, incremental, intentional actions in each area help us to do our part in pursuing the growth and change God wants for our lives.

Deep down, I think you know you have to take some kind of action in order to live out your dreams. The challenge is to switch your focus from changing your circumstances to changing yourself. Too often, people who genuinely want to experience change focus only on the externals. They'll change friends, change jobs, and even change churches, but they still end up feeling stuck and unfulfilled. If you find yourself thinking that your circumstances are the only thing holding you back, look out! It won't be long before the same old problems begin to show up in your new circumstances.

Leo Tolstoy once said, "Everyone thinks of changing humanity and nobody thinks of changing himself." I have my own saying: "Wherever you are, there *you* are!" When you change all of the externals but nothing in your life seems to turn around, *you* are the only thing left to change. Unless there's a different you, then nothing is really different.

Internal change always precedes external change. This is why people who have never had their minds renewed by God struggle all of their lives with the same issues and problems. They'll come to church week after week only to get up afterward, walk out the door, and chase their temptations and self-defeating habits all over again. Even if they buy all the books, attend all the self-help seminars, and take notes on all the sermons, they'll never experience a fulfilling sense of purpose and a future worth pursuing until they allow God to change them from the inside out. There's no substitute for that. You have to *be* before you can *do*. To be free to pursue your future, you must submit to the idea that God alone can renew your mind—change you on the inside—and take you where you were meant to be. One person who understands this truth is a woman from Indiana named Lori Mangrum.

Lori still remembers the night she woke up gasping for breath, her heart racing. When she tried to stand, she was overwhelmed by nausea and collapsed on the floor. It was the first in a series of debilitating panic attacks. The attacks eventually got so bad she couldn't risk even a drive to the grocery store.

A medical exam revealed that Lori had a heart condition that contributed to the attacks, but that wasn't the only cause of her anxiety. For years, Lori had been a "fixer," always working to solve other people's problems and ignoring her own. Her physician recommended counseling and prescribed anti-anxiety medication.

In her work with a Christian counselor, Lori discovered that solving other people's problems made her feel loved and accepted. She wanted to be seen as strong and competent. On the inside, however, her stress level was off the charts. Here's how Lori recalls her turning point:

I was driving home one afternoon following a session with my counselor, feeling so overwhelmed at the reality of my situation and utterly hopeless. I cried out to God, "I can't do this alone, it's too hard. If you're really there, then show me, and I will trust you!"

In the stillness, God's answer was clear: "Trust me first—then I will show you." And he did.[2]

Lori realized that the Lord never intended for her to be strong and competent every moment. She began focusing more on pleasing Him instead of everyone else. She learned to say no when she didn't want to do something, and to speak up when she felt angry or scared. The biggest change was in Lori's marriage. She began sharing more of her desires, thoughts, and fears with her husband, leading them both into a more intimate relationship. The panic attacks and her fear of the attacks began to diminish. Slowly but steadily, Lori changed from a woman tormented by anxiety into the joyful, trusting woman God designed her to be. When she allowed God to renew her mind—to change her on the inside—all the other good changes in her life naturally followed.

As you begin this journey to a new future, I challenge you to look inside yourself first. Before you try to change anything about your circumstances, allow God to help you identify the internal changes you need to pursue. Soak yourself in the truths of God's Word and allow God to renew your mind. That's the only way you can grow and break out of your old life. It's also the only way to prepare yourself for what comes next: a commitment to saying yes to whatever God asks of you.

Say Yes to Whatever God Asks of You

It has been said that people change when one of two things happens—they learn enough that they *want* to change, or they hit bottom hard enough that they *have* to change. In my case, on that long-ago night in Columbus, it was definitely a "have to" situation. When I grabbed hold of that light pole and gasped what I thought were my dying breaths, I grabbed hold of much, much more—a God who was ready to show me a whole new life.

Just a few months after the attack, I was at home on a Saturday morning when something remarkable happened. I was on my knees and praying when I suddenly had the surprising but definite sense that God was speaking to me. It wasn't an audible voice, yet I heard it loud and clear. "Bill," the voice said, "will you preach?"

This was just about the craziest idea I could imagine. I was eighteen years old, didn't know anything about preaching, and didn't have anyone in my family who'd ever preached. In all honesty, the "calling" I received that day freaked me out. And I didn't want to preach. Not because I was running from God, but because I felt it was far too great a responsibility. I was the last person anyone would imagine preaching. Only a few months earlier, I'd spent my Sundays carousing. I couldn't think of anyone less qualified to preach than I was. I felt certain that either I was either hearing things or God had crossed His wires somewhere.

Fortunately, I had a very effective technique for dealing with communication problems like this. If someone said something I didn't want to hear, I just talked louder and drowned them out. So I tried it with God.

"Lord, I'll do anything You want me to do," I prayed in a loud voice.

"Will you preach?"

Believe it or not, I tried to cut God off. "Lord," I said even louder, "I'll do anything You want me to do."

"Will you preach?"

It finally sank in that I was not going to be able to drown out a message from God. I gave in. "Yes, Lord," I said. "If You want me to preach, I'll preach."

A feeling of relief immediately washed over me. And then there was nothing more—God had stopped talking. *This is cool,* I thought. *I said yes, but I don't have a message or a place to preach. God just wanted to know if I was willing.*

I felt great! Everything was perfect—for about three hours.

That afternoon, my mother was in the kitchen washing dishes. She looked out the window and said, "There's the pastor." I looked too and, sure enough, there he was getting out of his car and walking toward our house. He'd never been to our home before. Other than a brief meeting at church, I'd never even spoken to him.

Oh, God, I thought. *What in the world are You doing?*

"I wonder what he wants?" my mother said. I hadn't said anything about my prayer experience earlier that day.

"He wants me to preach," I said.

My mother laughed. "Yeah, I'm sure he does," she said.

"No, I'm serious. You watch and see."

She looked at me, trying to figure out if I was joking. "You're crazy," she said.

A minute later, the pastor was sitting in our living room, and I was afraid of what he was going to say.

"Bill," he said, "I've had an emergency in my family, and I've got to go to Birmingham. A few hours ago, I was praying about who I could get to preach for me tomorrow. I felt strongly that I was supposed to ask if you would share your story and talk about your salvation."

I stared at him. My mother stared at me.

"I know I'm supposed to say yes," I said, "but I've never done that before. I've never stood up in front of people like that. God spoke to me about preaching a few hours ago, but I never thought it would happen this fast."

"Will you do it?" the pastor asked.

I swallowed. "I will."

I stayed up that whole night trying to prepare. I felt like I'd read the whole Bible through and couldn't find a sermon in it anywhere! Exhausted, I finally focused on a passage in Psalm 70 and went to sleep.

The next morning, I sat in the front pew, scared to death and still not believing I was doing this, when the music director said, "After we finish this song, a young man, one of our college students, is going to come up here and speak."

I could feel the sweat forming on my forehead. *Oh man,* I thought. *I hope they sing fifty verses of this song.*

Before I knew it, I had a microphone clipped to my shirt and was facing a crowd of nearly two hundred people. My plan was to say a few words about a couple of verses, then go into my story. I asked the congregation to turn to Psalm 70. They all knew their Bibles and found the passage quickly. Unfortunately, I was so nervous that I couldn't find it—anywhere!

I was shaking like a leaf. I think I even tore a page in my Bible. I wanted to die. I kept turning pages, looking frantically, while they all sat there with Psalm 70 opened in front of them, waiting on me.

Not knowing that the microphone they'd put on me would pick up the slightest sound, I whispered to myself, "Oh, God, just like the devil, he stole the Psalms out of my Bible!" The whole place erupted in laughter. I was mortified.

In desperation, I flipped more pages, found myself in the second book of Timothy, and said, "The Lord is leading me to another passage." I asked everybody to turn there with me. I butchered whatever message I tried to get across on those verses and quickly moved into the story of the stabbing, my encounter with God, and what He meant to me. The whole thing took less than fifteen minutes. At the end, I gave an invitation to come to Jesus unlike any I've heard before or since. "Look," I said, "if you want what I've got, come get it."

But here's the crazy thing—people started coming. They got out of those pews and walked down the aisle, many of them weeping with brokenness. Our church had never experienced that kind of revival. I stood there feeling shocked and exhausted, wondering, *What is going on in this place?*

People stood around celebrating God, and I was bewildered. Several approached me and said, "God has called you, young man."

When I went home that afternoon and thought about what happened, I couldn't believe it. Somehow, my words and my experience with God touched those people and made them want to know Him. I couldn't take any credit for it—God had led me every step of the way.

All I'd done was say yes to what He'd asked me to do. Pastor and author Pete Wilson says, "People say, 'I'm ready, willing, and able,' when all God needs is the willing part."[3] I experienced it firsthand that day.

I also knew just as certain as I knew my name that God had shown me His path to my destiny. It was going to be exciting and rewarding, and yes, it would be scary, too. Change always is. But if I kept growing closer to Him and kept saying yes to whatever He asked of me, He would lead the way. As someone once said, "You can trust a known God with an unknown future."

You can trust God with your future, too. If you make it your priority to grow in knowing God, allow Him to renew your mind, and say yes to whatever He asks you to do, you will be amazed at what He sends your way. A few years ago, I witnessed a beautiful demonstration of what it looks like to live this way when I was a guest speaker at a church convention. After the host introduced me, a man in the audience stood and said, "Yes, Lord." Then another stood and said, "Yes, Lord." All over that place, people stood and said, "Yes, Lord," again and again. When the last one had finished, the host turned to me and said, "Pastor Bill, we've already told the Lord our response to what He leads you to tell us, so come and give us our divine assignment."

I think that's a powerful example of what God would like from you and me—to say yes to Him before we even get our assignment and to trust completely in His plans for our destiny.

Insights for Inspiration

- When we stop growing, we stop living.

- Too often, we give in to pressure to conform.

- Change can be an exchange, an opportunity to trade up for something better.

- Through relationship with God, we allow Him to transform us by renewing our minds.

- When we say yes to whatever God asks, He will lead us to our destiny.

Verse to Review

"Therefore, if anyone is in Christ, the new creation has come: The old has gone, the new is here!" (2 Cor. 5:17 NIV).

Getting Personal

- Think back over the last day or two. What small or large opportunities did you have to take a risk for growth? For example, by being vulnerable, risking rejection or criticism, or choosing short-term pain for long-term gain. Did you respond more like a crab or a chameleon? Why?

- When you think of the places where you feel stuck or dissatisfied, how would you describe your efforts to make changes? Have you tended to focus more on changing your circumstances or on changing yourself?

- What would change in your life if you said yes to God more often? In what ways might these changes be "trading up," leading you closer to the life you want?

Dressing for Destiny

If you abide in Me, and My words abide in you,
ask whatever you wish, and it will be done for you.
John 15:7

You've come with me this far, so I hope that means you're willing to give this change process a chance. You are ready to grow closer to God, and you understand that you have to allow Him to renew your mind and you have to commit to saying yes to Him in order to discover your destiny. Now I hope you're asking, "What's next?" If so, I have one word for you: *prayer.*

Before I was stabbed, I'd never prayed. The whole idea of talking to an invisible God and expecting Him to hear me, let alone talk back to me, seemed a little far-fetched. But once I opened my eyes to God's presence in my life, my thinking changed. I found I had a deep hunger to talk to God.

Shortly after I came home from the hospital, this verse caught my attention: "But thou, when thou prayest, enter into thy closet, and when thou hast shut thy door, pray to thy Father which is in secret; and thy Father which seeth in secret shall reward thee openly" (Matt. 6:6 KJV). I was a literalist in those days, and if God wanted me to pray in a closet, that was just what I was going to do! I put a pillow on the floor in my bedroom closet, closed the door, dropped to my knees, and prayed to God.

You have to understand, this was not a casual effort. I was like a poker player pushing every chip to the middle of the table—I was all in. Sometimes I prayed from six in the evening until one in the morning. Sometimes I prayed all night. I know my mother was thrilled that my faith in God had taken off, but I think she must have wondered if I was secretly still drinking or doing drugs in there. She even talked to our pastor about her concerns. In what they thought was helpful guidance, they both kindly informed me that I didn't have to pray so long or so much, that God loved me just the same.

I wasn't drinking or doing drugs, of course. I just had a deep hunger to connect with God in prayer. And even though I wasn't praying for the reward that verse talks about, I sure didn't expect what happened, which felt more like a punishment. Once I started praying, it was like God cut me off from people. Before I gave my life to Christ, I'd had a lot of friends and always enjoyed my social life. But my old friends were part of my past, and I had no new friends who shared my faith. Even worse, when it came to dating, I suddenly felt like I was invisible to the opposite sex. I couldn't get a date no matter how hard I tried.

At times, I argued with God about it. "God, why is it that guys who treat girls badly can still find a date," I said, "and here I am on another Friday night in my prayer closet with You? As much as I love Your presence in my life and the salvation You've given me, why have You cut off my social life completely?"

I dreaded weekends because I had nowhere to go except church on Sundays, and even that was lonely. I loved the pastor and I soaked up every sermon, but the students in the college-aged group had been in church all their lives. They weren't comfortable with someone like me and didn't include me in their conversations. I felt like a cantaloupe in a watermelon patch—I just didn't fit in.

My time of intense prayer and no social life lasted for nearly three years. It was a very discouraging period of my life. But as I look back on those days now, I realize that God knew exactly what He was doing. He was separating me from distractions so I could learn to recognize His voice and rely on Him from the very beginning of our relationship.

We all go through dry stretches in our lives and our relationship with God. These are the times when answers don't come easily—or come at all—and we feel like our prayers fall flat. What I try to remember when this happens is that there are seasons in the spiritual life. Just as corn and wheat don't grow year-round, we won't always have the experience of bountiful harvest in the spiritual life. There are seasons for planting and seasons for reaping. If I'm facing hard times, it doesn't mean God has abandoned me or that He doesn't love me. I may just be in a season of sowing seeds for a future harvest. Even though I'd love to see instant answers to my prayers, I've learned that it's during those times when I'm forced to struggle and wait that my faith, my spiritual roots, and my maturity grow most.

This was the case when my social life dried up. I didn't like the season I was going through, but it anchored me in God like nothing else could have. I *needed* those three lonely years to focus only on God, to discover who He was and how much He loved me, and to learn how to depend on Him. If I'd been hanging out with friends, going on dates, and filling my days with activity, I might easily have missed God and never experienced the relationship we both wanted.

God wants that same kind of relationship with you. And He's created you with a deep desire for friendship with Him and with other human beings. Just look at Jesus. When Jesus came to earth, He spent His time building relationships with ordinary people. He stopped in the midst of a crowd to give attention to a sick woman. He neglected food to talk to an adulterous woman at a well. He invited Himself to a tax collector's house. He confounded the most brilliant minds of His day, and yet "the common people heard him gladly" (Mark 12:37 KJV). In every case, Jesus was concerned about building relationships with people. He once said to His disciples, "I no longer call you slaves. . . . Now you are my friends" (John 15:15 NLT). If you want to pursue your God-given destiny, you have to have that kind of intimate friendship with God—and prayer is the best thing you can do to build and strengthen that relationship.

Sometimes people wonder why we need to pray if God already knows everything about us, including what we need, what we desire, and what we fear. We pray because as we talk with God and listen to God, we get to know God better. Can you imagine having a close relationship with someone if you only talked to them when you needed something? As we share our lives with God—expressing our joys, our desires, our gratitude, or our fears—we demonstrate our desire for a relationship with God for who He is, not just for what we hope He will do for us.

Most parents understand this concept. I can always tell when my oldest son is discouraged or has something on his mind. Usually B.J. has more energy than the Energizer Bunny. He's always talking, laughing, and happy. So when he's quiet and withdrawn, I know something is up. But I don't swoop in like Superdad and try to fix his problems. I wait for him to talk with me. In fact, I long for him to open his heart to me. Nothing brings us closer than a father-son heart-to-heart, and few things make my heart gladder than when my son trusts me, depends on me, and respects me enough to share his life with me.

Your heavenly Father feels the same way about you. He wants to enjoy intimate conversations with His children. He longs for you to know His love and concern for you, and He wants to talk with you and share life with you every day.

Two Reasons Prayer Is Essential

When we get to know God on an intimate level through prayer, we have access to the only true source of joy and peace. We have a spiritual guide, protector, and friend who is available to help us right now, no matter what problem we face. But the benefit is long-term as well. A relationship with God based on prayer equips us with two critical skills that enable us to move closer to our destiny. In prayer, we learn to hear God's voice, and we are trained for battle readiness.

Learning to Hear God's Voice

Learning to hear and recognize God's voice is often like listening to an old-style radio while taking a long-distance trip in your car. The farther you drive, the more likely it is that your favorite station will be interrupted by other voices or static. You have to readjust the dial to get rid of the noise and stay tuned in to the station you want. To navigate life change in a world filled with noisy distractions, we must learn how to recognize—and stay tuned in to—the Father's voice above the rest.

My youngest son, Blake, had a hernia operation when he was just three years old. When the surgery team took Blake away, a nurse told Debbie and me that his operation wouldn't begin for several hours, so we settled ourselves in the waiting room with other parents. Twenty minutes later, we heard a young child cry. Debbie immediately jumped up, said, "That's Blake," and rushed out of the waiting room. I looked at the other parents and felt like apologizing for my overanxious wife. Then Debbie came back and said, "His doctor is calling us, Bill."

"We went ahead and took him first," the doctor said, "and he's going to be fine now." As we walked back to the recovery room, I had to ask Debbie, "With all of the other children crying in this busy children's hospital, how did you know that cry came from Blake?"

"Mothers know the voice of their children," Debbie said matter-of-factly. I was amazed. *How come I hadn't recognized the sound of my son's cry?* To me, it just blended in with the rest of the squalls. Here's the point. Prayer helps us develop something like a mother's ears. When we routinely spend time with God each day, we learn to distinguish the voice of God from all the other voices squalling for our attention.

Here's another example. Do you know how bank tellers are trained to detect counterfeit currency? You might think they spend a lot of time studying counterfeits, right? But they don't. Instead, they study the real deal. They spend days with genuine dollar bills—studying them, feeling them, listening to the way they sound when handled, even smelling them. When they come across a counterfeit, they know it. Because of their familiarity with the real thing, they're quick to notice a fake.

That's how prayer works for you and me—it gives us a way to spend time with the real thing. When we pray regularly, we're quicker to hear God's voice, to discern truth from error, and also to get the spiritual nutrition we need. This is why the Bible tells us, "But you, beloved, building yourselves up on your most holy faith, praying in the Holy Spirit, *keep yourselves in the love of God*, waiting anxiously for the mercy of our Lord Jesus Christ to eternal life" (Jude vv. 20–21, emphasis added). Prayer is one of the most effective tools we have to keep ourselves in the love of God—to be bonded with Him and attentive to His leadership. It prepares us to move in the right direction when He points us toward our destiny.

In those formative months when I spent so many hours in my prayer closet, I developed not only a deeper bond with God but also a greater gift of discernment. And it wasn't long until I had a chance to put that discernment into practice. I'd been a Christian only a few months and was attending church with my sister Sonja and her family. Their pastor was about forty years old, married with three children, and well liked. Each time I attended church, he invited me to return in the evening for a mentoring session he led with college-aged young men.

It was an honor to be invited into this group, and there was a part of me that really wanted this man's affirmation and approval, but I found myself repeatedly declining his invitations. Although I couldn't say exactly why at first, I felt uneasy about him. This man had once been a youth pastor and knew how to connect with young people, but I'd heard stories that didn't sit well with me. For example, he had a reputation for playing pranks, including humiliating young men before their wedding day by "pantsing" them with the help of other guys. That kind of behavior in a leader did not seem proper, but I was new at this whole Christianity thing so I kept quiet.

One Sunday when my sister and I went to church, a man I'd never seen before stood in front of the congregation and announced that the pastor had been dismissed. He'd been caught in acts of sexual misconduct with several of the young men he was mentoring.

I was disappointed and disillusioned. *What happened? How could a pastor do this?* It was a game-changing day for me. That evening, I went by myself into a field, sat down by a tree, and prayed: "God, I don't know how serious everybody else is about their faith, but I know that what You did for me is real. So even if everybody in the world walks away from You at some point, I will always remember what You did for me. I will not give up my walk with You for anyone. I refuse to be starstruck by others. I will honor and respect everyone, but I will not trade my real experience with You for the recognition or acceptance of someone else."

You could say that this was the day I dropped my spiritual anchor. It was only because of all those months of prayer that I was protected from distraction and able to discern what was happening when the need for discernment came. My love for God and understanding of His love for me allowed me to trust His voice and rest in His care and protection. As I look back over the years on all the wonderful changes God has brought about in me and through me as I've tried to follow His plans for my future, I see that those plans were possible only because I learned to hear and trust God's voice through prayer.

Training for Battle Readiness

I live near Fort Benning, Georgia. This army base is known around the world for being one of the largest and best for training and preparing soldiers. Many of those who live and train there, from the highest-ranking officers to the new recruits, attend our church. One significant trait they all share is that they are ready at all times. These dedicated men and women remind me of a statement made by one of my favorite mixed martial arts fighters, Urijah Faber: "If you stay ready, you don't have to rush out to get ready."[1] It's a truth that applies just as much to spiritual life as it does to military life. The more we pray, the more God begins to change us and get us ready for the challenges we'll soon face.

As in just about everything, Jesus is our example when it comes to relying on prayer to prepare us for what lies ahead. When Jesus was about to choose His disciples, He spent most of the previous night in prayer (Luke 6:12–16). He sometimes prayed early in the morning (Mark 1:35) and often went off by Himself to pray (Matt. 14:23). Before He went to the cross, Jesus spent a night in prayer so intense He sweat drops of blood (Luke 22:44). Jesus made prayer a lifestyle, and it's clear that He was always in "ready mode" as a result.

That kind of spiritual training and preparation is vital if we hope to overcome the challenges we'll face as we seek to change and live out the destiny God has for us. Too often we lose these battles—and fail to move on to the next phase in God's plan for us—simply because we've neglected the foundational spiritual training we need. Just like the soldiers at Fort Benning, we have to train if we want to be ready for battle. In his letter to the church at Ephesus, the apostle Paul describes how to prepare for this kind of battle readiness:

> Therefore, take up the full armor of God, so that you will be able to resist in the evil day, and having done everything, to stand firm. Stand firm therefore, having girded your loins with truth, and having put on the breastplate of righteousness, and having shod your feet with the preparation of the gospel of peace; in addition to all, taking up the shield of faith with which you will be able to extinguish all the flaming arrows of the evil one. And take the helmet of salvation, and the sword of the Spirit, which is the word of God. With all prayer and petition pray at all times in the Spirit. (Ephesians 6:13–18)

To stay ready for battle, we put on the armor of God. And an important element of His armor is prayer. You could say that when we put on our spiritual armor—absorb God's truth through His Word and through prayer—we are dressing for our destiny.

My family says that I am calm in a crisis. If that's true, I will be the first to confess it's not something that comes naturally to me. I'm just as capable as the next guy of quickly losing my temper or my composure, and when I do, the result doesn't honor God or move me closer to His plan for my future. Most of the time, though, I stay calm. Why? Because I have put on the armor of God through prayer. I remember that nothing can upset His plans and that He has control of the situation. When I rest in that truth, it's as if the "arrows" coming my way just bounce off. Prayer keeps me rooted in God's will for my life, encouraged in spite of distractions, and ready to face whatever comes next.

A Way to Pray

Maybe I've convinced you that prayer is important, but as with me before my encounter with God, the whole idea of conversing with your Creator still makes you uncomfortable. Or it could be that you've never really prayed before, and you're not sure how to go about it. Wherever you're at, if you're ready to learn to pray, I think I can help you with that.

It doesn't make much difference whether you pray on your knees or standing up, aloud or in a quiet voice. You don't have to use impressive words or speak in religious jargon. The secret is not necessarily in how long you pray. If your friend prayed for an hour this morning and you prayed for twenty minutes, it doesn't mean your friend is more spiritual than you are. Just talk with God. That's what's important. Even if it feels awkward at first, know that God is pleased even by your desire to communicate with Him. God wants to hear what's on your heart, and He wants to respond to it.

One of the most helpful structures for prayer I know uses the acronym ACTIP:

Adoration
Confession
Thanksgiving
Intercession
Petitions

Let's take a closer look at each one.

Adoration

Whenever people in the Bible approached a king or a member of royalty, it was important that they first showed honor and respect. They would bow and say something like, "Oh king, may you live forever." You might recall that this is how the prophet Daniel addressed King Darius from the den of lions (Dan. 6:21). It was a sign of respect and recognition of the king's authority.

When He taught His disciples to pray what we now call the Lord's Prayer, Jesus began in a similar way: "Our Father who is in heaven, hallowed be Your name" (Matt. 6:9). Other translations have, "may your name be kept holy," or "help us to honor your name." When we honor God in this way, we express not only our respect, but also our love for Him. That's what adoration is—a loving high regard for who God is and for the legitimate authority He has over our lives. It moves the heart of God when we adore Him.

I often open my prayers with such words as, "Father, there is none like You. I honor You. I worship You. I am honored that You allow me to pray." But don't copy me when you pray. Prayer isn't a formula. Speak from your heart, reflect on God's blessings, and allow your adoration for God to flow.

Confession

Sin is deeply offensive to God—and we've all sinned (Rom. 3:23). Fortunately, we've also all been offered the opportunity to be saved from God's wrath by Jesus. I sometimes explain it this way. Imagine you're standing in the middle of a road and a nearby dam suddenly bursts. Millions of tons of water are flooding in your direction. You have no chance to survive this onslaught. But at the last instant, a man steps in front of you and somehow blocks the terrible force of all that water. You're saved by this heroic act, but the man loses his life. This is something like what Jesus did for you and me when He died on the cross. He bridged the gap between God and us by taking on Himself the punishment for our sins.

Though Jesus has intervened on our behalf, God still hates sin. The psalmist once wrote, "If I regard iniquity in my heart, the Lord will not hear me" (Ps. 66:18 KJV). What that means is, if we take sin lightly or cherish it in our hearts, it offends God. We have to take sin seriously, and we do that by confessing it.

Confession is an honest admission of guilt. It includes being truly sorry for sin as well as making a sincere resolution to avoid committing this sin again. In confession, we acknowledge the specifics of our sin, refusing to generalize, justify, or gloss over the truth about what we have done or left undone. Then we receive God's forgiveness and thank Him for it. We ask for His help to change our ways and to apologize or make restitution to anyone we may have harmed. Routinely confessing sins in this way keeps us in right relationship with God and others because it keeps pride and rebellion from ever taking root.

Your confession might be as simple as this: "Dear God, I confess that I haven't listened to other people as attentively as I could have. I don't want You to listen to me in the same manner in which I've listened to them. I've let busyness and activity distract me. Thanks for Your forgiveness and understanding. Please help me to be more attentive and in-the-moment the next time I enter into conversation with those around me." When you are willing to humble yourself before our all-knowing, all-loving Father and admit that you've stumbled, He will always be there to pick you up, offer His forgiveness, and help you grow in the process.

Thanksgiving

As I write this, I have a grandson who is just learning to talk. My son asked me what words I thought they should teach him first. My answer? "Teach him how to say 'thank you.' I know people forty years old who still haven't learned how to say those two words."

My grandson will go a long way in life if he can learn not just to use those words as a social formality, but to really mean them. The same will be true for you when you make it a habit to express your sincere gratitude to God.

In thanksgiving, we remember what God has done for us—provisions small and large, recent and ongoing, personal and corporate. Just as specificity is important for confession, we want to be specific in expressing our gratitude.

> *Thank You, Lord, for giving me a job that enables me to provide for my family.*
> *Thank You for giving me the courage to apologize to my coworker.*
> *Thank You for the beautiful sound of my child's laughter.*
> *Thank You for the rain that watered my garden last night.*
> *Thank You for loving me no matter what.*

When we routinely and sincerely thank God for who He is and for all He's done for us, it resets our hearts and fosters a grateful mindset. It's actually part of how God renews our minds so we can think His thoughts and see the world the way He does. That's why the Bible tells us, "Devote yourselves to prayer, keeping alert in it with an attitude of thanksgiving" (Col. 4:2). Thanksgiving is life changing!

Intercession

Intercession is a big word that simply means praying on behalf of others. When the apostle Peter was in prison, "the church was earnestly praying to God for him" (Acts 12:5 NIV). That's intercession. The apostle Paul repeatedly engaged in intercession for believers in the churches he visited: "I thank my God in all my remembrance of you, always offering prayer with joy in my every prayer for you all" (Phil. 1:3–4). When we pray for the sick (James 5:14), pray for our enemies (Matt. 5:44), and pray for those in authority (1 Tim. 2:1–2), we are interceding for them.

Praying for one another in this way not only expands our hearts and helps us to see beyond our own limited concerns but also bonds us with those we're praying for. When we pray earnestly for others, we join them in their struggles and help them to carry their burdens (Gal. 6:2). And there is power in this kind of prayer. God is moved to act when His children pray to Him on behalf of others. Don't miss out on securing these blessings or allowing God the opportunity to change *you* in the process. When you focus on others, God is at work in you, renewing your mind, removing self-centered tendencies, and increasing your compassion for others.

So what does intercession look like? Perhaps you might ask a coworker how you can pray for him that day and then follow through: "Lord, please help Michael to finish his research report on time today. Give him the insight and wisdom he needs to make recommendations that will help our business to be more effective." Or you might pray for your spouse and kids: "Dear God, I ask that You guide my husband to a new job that will better utilize his people skills. And please help my son to make good friends at his new school." You might commit to praying weekly for the members of your Bible study group. Or you can intercede for your pastors and other church leaders. Those prayers are never wasted!

Years ago, we began a Pastor's Prayer Partner ministry after hearing author John Maxwell describe how a man named Bill Klauson started that ministry for him. I knew I needed the help that would come from the power of prayer. It's the foundation of every success we've enjoyed as a church. I now have over 1,100 partners praying for me. During prayer time at our services each week, our prayer partners come together in a designated spot to pray for me and my family and for other needs in our church family. For over twenty years, this team has lifted my hands and encouraged my heart. Together, we've experienced favor on top of favor from God because of it.

Are you beginning to see how important prayer is to becoming the person God made you to be? All the components of prayer we've covered so far—adoration, confession, thanksgiving, and intercession—create opportunities for God to transform your mind and heart.

Petitions

My wife will tell you that I am no fun to go shopping with. On a trip to the mall, my only useful function is supplying the cash. You see, Debbie likes to window shop. She enjoys strolling through each and every store we pass, looking at items, picking them up, sampling them. It's the worst when she takes me with her to go shoe shopping. She'll gather up a dozen different shoes from the displays and hand them to a clerk who then disappears into the stockroom before returning with a dozen boxes. Then, of course, it's time for Debbie to try them all on, one by one, heel by heel, lace by lace. That's followed by the obligatory strut down the aisle to see if the shoes fit right, feel comfortable, and, most importantly, look good. I take my spot in a chair next to a handful of other men who are patiently fulfilling their marital shopping duties and do my best to be supportive. I tell Debbie which shoes I like and which ones I don't while she boxes up each pair and heads to the checkout counter. She hands them to the same overworked clerk, who asks, "Did any of these work for you today?"

That's when I hold my breath, waiting to hear how many boxes are coming home with us and what the financial damages will be. But inevitably I hear something like this from Debbie instead: "I can't decide because I'm not sure exactly what I'm looking for. I'll probably be back tomorrow."

That's my wife. She likes to window shop. At least window shopping is inexpensive!

On the other hand, if I'm going to shop, you can bet your hat I'll be bringing something home. I don't shop to browse. I shop to buy. If I go into a shoe store, I come out with a pair of shoes—not just any shoes, but the exact pair I went in to purchase. If I came in for loafers, I'll leave with loafers. If I came in for, gulp, flip-flops, I'll leave with . . . something else. I hate flip-flops. The point is that I know what I want, and I don't leave the store without it.

When it comes to prayers of petition, I always encourage people to pray like I shop—with focus and determination. A petition is a request. In prayer, we petition God to provide for us or to take action on our behalf. We ask him to meet our needs, be they physical, emotional, spiritual, financial, or relational. When you make your petitions, don't pray like a window shopper, aimlessly wandering through your conversation with God, hoping He'll read between the lines and catch one or two random requests you throw out amidst the fluff. It drives me crazy to hear people pray who keep circling the airport and never land the plane. Simply ask God for what you need and be specific.

Even though God wants us to ask for what we need, I know people who have unmet needs at least in part because they don't believe they have the right to ask for them. "God doesn't have time to take care of such a small need as that," they tell themselves. "He's got bigger problems than mine. I'd just be wasting His time." Yet the Bible says, "You do not have because you do not ask" (James 4:2). What if all you have to do is ask? It's not that God is concerned only about the big things. He's concerned with anything that concerns you. Scripture says, "Cast all your anxiety on him because he cares for you" (1 Peter 5:7 NIV).

If you're frustrated with your life and have a nagging sense that God created you for something more, petition God about those concerns. Ask God to lead you into your unique destiny. Pray for His preparation in your life, and ask for the patience to wait for His leading. Ask for the wisdom to recognize any doors He opens for you, as well as the courage to step through them when they open. Above all, acknowledge that God's plans are more important to you than your own plans. Whatever your petitions, be willing to pray with Christ, "Not my will, but yours be done" (Luke 22:42 NIV). That is the clearest path I know for fast-tracking yourself to the destiny God has for you.

I find the ACTIP method helpful for covering all the bases when I pray, but you certainly don't have to take the same approach. God isn't concerned about your prayer style or how many big words you use. Like anyone who loves you, He just wants to talk with you on a regular basis. However you do it, just make sure you spend time with God and get to know Him. He's waiting to hear from you.

Prayer does more than develop our relationship with God, however. It also connects us to His divine power—power that can propel us into our destiny.

The Power of Prayer

I have seen the miraculous power of prayer countless times, both in my own life and in the lives of others. One of those times took place after our first Mother's Day service back in 1983. A dark-haired woman in her late twenties sat in the second row and cried quietly throughout the service. My initial thought was, *Her mother must have died recently. I'm preaching on Mother's Day, and this is a painful time for her.*

When the service was over, the young woman walked up to me and said, "I know you must have seen me crying."

"I did," I said. "Did you lose your mother?"

"No," she said. "I can't have a baby. I've been to doctor after doctor, and I can't have a child. A Mother's Day service is always painful for people like me."

This doesn't happen to me often, but in that moment I sensed the Lord giving me a clear directive: "Pray for her to have a child."

Lord, I thought, *didn't You just hear? She says she can't have a baby.* The last thing I wanted to do was give false hope to a hurting young woman. Yet I knew what I'd heard, and I knew I'd be disobeying God if I didn't follow His instructions.

I gently put my arm around the woman's shoulders and said, "If it's all right, let me pray for you." She nodded and I prayed. "Father, I want to thank You for the baby You're going to send to Teresa. I thank You that You're going to open her womb and give her a child."

I wish I could say I prayed with great faith, but it was more a prayer of obedience. I couldn't help wondering if I'd only made her situation worse.

A few months later, Teresa came up to me after a service. "Miracle of miracles!" she said. "I'm pregnant. My husband and I are expecting a baby."

I was thrilled for her and congratulated her. Later, I sensed the Lord telling me that this prayer miracle wasn't over. "From this moment on," He said, "I want you to pray every Mother's Day for women who want a child but have been told they can't have one."

For more than thirty years now, I've asked couples and women desiring a child to come forward on Mother's Day so we as a church can pray for them. *Every single one* of those years, at least one woman—and sometimes more—who'd been told she couldn't have a baby became pregnant during the following year. Today, many of these women join with me at the front of the church to pray for those who are struggling as they once did. It's one of the most amazing things we've ever been privileged to participate in as a church—and it's all because of the power of prayer.

And if you want to see the power of prayer at work in changing someone's destiny, look no further than my friend Eric. Eric had a passion for planes and had always wanted to work in the aviation industry. But the doors had always closed for him, perhaps in part because he'd been confined to a wheelchair from birth. It didn't help matters that Eric had never even lived outside of Columbus, Georgia, which is not exactly the aviation capital of the world.

Before giving up, Eric realized that he needed to take his aspirations to God in a more strategic way. He began praying and fasting every Tuesday, dedicating hours to talking with God about his desire to work in aviation.

Apparently, a career in aviation was God's plan for Eric, too, because just a few weeks later, he received an unexpected phone call. A year before, he'd sent his résumé to Southwest Airlines and then forgotten about it when he never got a response. Now they were calling! Would he be interested, they asked, in coming out to Texas for an interview? He certainly was. The interview went well—so well that they said, "You're exactly what we're looking for!" Today, Eric has an administrative position with Southwest in the Dallas–Fort Worth area. He has no doubt that he is living out his dream thanks to the power of prayer.

Every week before I deliver a sermon at church, I sit down in my office to pray (yes, I have moved beyond my bedroom closet!). I close my eyes and pray something like this: "God, I love these people, but not like You do. I don't know who's coming today, and I don't know what they're facing. They may be alone, and their world may be falling apart. They may be succeeding in life and wondering what the next step is.

God, for the next half hour while I speak, would You give me Your love for them?"

When I leave my office and walk into the church sanctuary, I look at people differently. As I walk toward the pulpit, I might hug an elderly woman and say, "It's so good to see you," or tell a teenager, "If you get any better looking, Hollywood's going to be coming for you." After that prayer in the office, my heart is full of love for the people I serve, and I believe it flows through me as I preach. It's just one small example of what prayer can do.

Do you have an intimate relationship with the Lord? Do you spend enough time with Him in prayer to recognize His voice throughout your day? Are you ready to dress for your destiny by putting on the spiritual armor that will prepare you for the battle and for your future? Are you willing to activate the power of God through prayer?

I hope so. Your destiny awaits.

Insights for Inspiration

- It's when we're forced to struggle and wait that we draw closer to God and deepen our spiritual roots.

- We can learn to hear and recognize God's voice when we spend time with Him in prayer.

- We often lose our battles in life—and fail to move on to the next phase in God's plan for us—because we've neglected our spiritual basic training.

- Prayer creates opportunities for God to transform our minds and our hearts.

Verse to Review

"So I say to you, ask, and it will be given to you; seek, and you will find; knock, and it will be opened to you" (Luke 11:9).

Getting Personal

- How would you describe the current level of your hunger to connect with God in prayer? Is it the highest it's ever been, the lowest, or somewhere in between?

- Think back over the last day or two. Were there any moments when you recognized God's voice prompting you? If not, when was the last time you heard God's voice? What did you sense God was saying? How did you respond?

- Which of the ACTIP components of prayer do you feel most interested in practicing or learning more about? Which, if any, make you uncomfortable? Why?

- In what area of your life do you most desire to experience the power of prayer?

Envisioning Your Future

The only limits are, as always, those of vision.
James Broughton

Three men were working on a construction site in Chicago. Curious to know how they felt about their work, a bystander approached and asked, "What are you doing?" The first worker replied, "Are you blind? I'm welding these steel beams and putting them together the way the boss tells me. My hands are bruised and cut, it's backbreaking work, and it's boring me to death."

The second worker replied, "I'm connecting these beams according to the architect's plans. It's hard work and sometimes repetitive, but I earn almost a thousand dollars a week. It's a decent job that allows me to support my family. Could be worse."

When the third worker replied, he pointed to the sky and said, "Can't you see? I'm building a hospital that will provide medical help for people all over the city!"

The first worker couldn't see anything in his work beyond how hard it was, the second couldn't see anything in his work beyond what he got out of it, but the third worker had vision. Vision is seeing past the present into the future. It's seeing things not as they are but as they could be.

Vision is one of the most important things you need to get from point A to point B. The Bible says, "Where there is no vision, the people perish" (Prov. 29:18 KJV). Without a clear understanding of where you want to be in life—and a passion to get there—your ability to grow and change will be limited. The good news is that God has a unique vision and plan for your future. The bad news is, unless you do your part to live into that vision, you may never discover it. God can be trusted to do His part if you do yours. He wants to walk with you as you discover His will for your life, and He will be with you every step of the way when you have the courage to live it out.

We all have dreams. We may dream of being a teacher who changes lives, a doctor who saves lives, or a musician who brings joy to life. We may dream of becoming a great friend or a loving spouse. But dreams can be fuzzy. Like our literal dreams during sleep that easily slip away when we wake up, the dreams we form in our imagination are sometimes hazy. We may have a vague sense of what it means to be a doctor and what it would take to become one, but we're not ready to act on the idea by studying chemistry and biology. This kind of dream is actually just wishful thinking.

Vision changes that. A vision is a concrete target that helps you break out of where you are so you can get to where you want to be. It helps you to keep reaching for your goals even when you hit obstacles and roadblocks. It gives you hope for a better future and the ability to see the possibilities in every circumstance. When you have a vision, you see yourself in the future you desire and believe that it can become reality. The best vision of all, of course, is the one that aligns with God's vision for you.

But you have to have clear sight lines to put your vision in focus. And just as with any journey, developing a vision begins with taking some first steps. You have to imagine the future, share the future, plan the future, create the future, and then risk the future.

Step 1: Imagine the Future

I once read that three quarters of working Americans are dissatisfied in their jobs. If you're in a similar situation, don't hang your head. Dissatisfaction can actually be a catalyst for change. Before you can step into God's vision of your future, you have to be dissatisfied with where you are today. I call it divine discontentment. It's just enough uneasiness to keep you continually reaching for the next level. The tragedy, however, is that few of those who are discontent ever take action to pursue what they say they want. Their actions say that they are satisfied being dissatisfied.

In today's fast-paced, success-oriented society, we invest countless hours in building careers and making a living, but we never seem to get ahead. Did you know that at the end of the day, the average person has thirty-six hours of unfinished work piled up somewhere? Here's what that means. If you're waiting around for more time, more finances, or more opportunity before you allow yourself to fulfill your future, it's never going to happen. You'll spend your life surviving rather than thriving. The only way to truly imagine your future is to schedule time to dream. It's your hopes and dreams that reveal what you're passionate about, call you to something more, and ultimately lead you into the future God has for you.

When I first met the woman who would become my wife, I had no idea what I was looking for in a girl. I didn't have a vision for what a serious relationship could be because I hadn't set aside time to dream about it. At that point, I'd had three solitary years of getting to know God, and when He opened the doors for me to date again, everything changed in a hurry. Suddenly, I was dating three attractive girls at once and had no time for anything else. You could tell by looking at my apartment. It was such a mess that I decided to hire someone to clean it on a regular basis.

Debbie was the girl who answered my ad for a housecleaner. She was a former homecoming queen with a beautiful smile, a direct and confident manner, and a respectful attitude. At the time, I wasn't even thinking about trying to date anyone new—I had my hands full already! First, I gave Debbie instructions on cleaning the house. Then I gave her instructions on the girls: "If Susan calls," I said, "tell her that we're still on for tonight. If Teresa calls, tell her we have tickets to the ball game Saturday. If Lisa calls, tell her I'll pick her up for lunch on Sunday." Debbie just took it all in, kept looking at my indoor junkyard, and raised her fee.

A few weeks later, my day of reckoning finally arrived. The three girls I was dating all started putting pressure on me for a more serious relationship. Our dates changed. Each time a love song came on the radio, one girl turned it up higher and asked me if I loved that song like she did. When another had to try on a bridesmaid dress, she wanted me to see it, and then she wandered over to look at wedding dresses too. The third girl asked me to go to her family reunion so I could meet the extended family. It felt like all three of them conspired together, each asking me to date her exclusively at the same time. I didn't know what to do.

I sought advice from a trusted friend, who gave me the best counsel: "Bill, you can't see the trees for the forest," he said. "Those are not the girls you need to date." I must have looked a little confused, so he went on to explain, "You should be dating the one who comes over and cleans your apartment. She's not chasing you, and she's not playing games. I've talked to all four of these girls—the three you're dating and the one you're not—and the one you're not dating is the best fit for you."

The more I thought about it, the more his words made sense to me. Over the next few weeks, I began talking to Debbie when she came over to clean, and I liked what I heard and observed in her. She was solid in her faith, consistently calm and confident, and not desperate for a man. She knew who she was and never tried to be anything else.

Suddenly, I had a vision for the kind of woman I wanted to spend the rest of my life with! And I knew exactly what I needed to do. I broke off dating the others and focused on Debbie. We hit it off, were married the next year, and have enjoyed more than thirty-five wonderful years together. Talk about living into God's destiny! Looking back now, I see how clearly God's vision for my life came as I waited, listened, and acted on what I sensed He was revealing. God didn't send Debbie to make my apartment better; He sent her to make my life better.

You too can discover and live out God's vision for your life. But you can't skip this first step of taking time to dream. Instead of asking questions like, "What am I *expected* to be?" or "What am I *allowed* to do?" start by asking yourself, "Where does God *want* me to be?" and "Who does God *want* me to be?" You have to think outside the box—beyond other people's expectations and your own self-imposed limits—before you can get outside the box.

One of the greatest visionaries I've ever known was the late bass-fishing legend Tom Mann. Early on in high school, I dated one of his daughters, became a dear friend to another, and was a close friend of his son, Tommy. I was sad but honored to conduct Tommy's funeral a few years ago. Tom Mann was a three-time world champion bass fisherman, inducted into the Professional Bass Fishing Hall of Fame, and the designer of incredibly popular lures. When I was in his home as a teenager, it was common to see famous people like President Jimmy Carter, Porter Wagoner, Dolly Parton, Joe Namath, the state governor, and college football coaches there.

Tom's late wife, Ann, once shared with me what it was like living with him. "Tom was a visionary," she said. "He'd get this idea in his head and keep thinking it over and over. Then he'd draw it out on the back of an old brown grocery sack. He'd get all excited and tell me how this would work, why people would line up for it, and then he'd plan it all out while I just listened. If I supported him—and I always did, I wasn't going to kill his dreams—he'd take that paper sack drawing and go get a legal patent on it. The next thing I knew, our whole family would be making his drawing a reality in our home living room assembly line. Me, Tommy, Sharon, Cindy, and little Nelda would paint, glue, dry, and wrap each lure." Tom Mann started his bass-fishing empire with a vision and a five-dollar business license. He went on to sell over a billion fishing lures, launch other related businesses, and change the world of fishing with his innovations.

What could you do if you really allowed yourself to be captivated by your visions the way Tom Mann was? Are you willing to find out?

You can start by setting aside time to be alone with God—and bringing along a pen and notepad (or your laptop). Prayerfully ask God to reveal His plans for you. As you wait for His guidance, take time to reflect on and respond—in writing—to questions like these:

- What do I enjoy doing most?
- What do I do best?
- If I could accomplish only one task in life, what would it be?
- What do I think about most?
- Who are three people I most respect? Why?
- What is my personality type? In what ways has God made me different and unique from others?

God may not choose to reveal His plan for you all at once, but as you continue to make your responses to these questions part of your prayer, you'll be taking steps in the direction of your dreams.

Once you've identified some of your hopes and dreams, let them marinate for a while before you rush out and try to make things happen. When you trust God enough to allow Him to transform your dreams into a vision, you give God the opportunity to lead—to show you the undeniable signs that He is preparing you. Continue to seek God's guidance through prayer and reading the Bible. If you know your vision is inspired by God from the beginning, you will have confidence to keep pressing forward when you encounter difficulties down the road—and you can be sure that you will encounter difficulties! When you think about giving up, you can go back and remember how and why you started. This will reignite your vision and your motivation.

Author and theologian Walter Russell Bowie once said, "The mightiest works have been accomplished by men who have somehow kept their ability to dream great dreams."[1] I have always believed that the best way to achieve a dream is to aim beyond it. If you want to play professional baseball, you should aim for the Hall of Fame. If you want to be a vice president, aim to be the president. It's like the story of two insurance representatives who set their sales goals at the beginning of a new year. One wrote down fifty thousand dollars on an index card and sealed it in an envelope. The other wrote down one million dollars and did the same. At the end of the year they opened their envelopes. The man who predicted fifty thousand dollars was elated, saying, "I hit my goal right on target!" His coworker looked down at his card and said, "I guess I only made it halfway to mine."

When you envision your future, allow yourself to see all the way to the horizon, no matter how far away it seems. The greatest barrier to vision is the misconception that God would never lead you to do something beyond what is already within your power to do. Tradition, fear, and mediocrity may slow you down, but the most devastating hindrances are limitations that are self-imposed. Don't allow your weaknesses or circumstances to limit your hopes or your imagination. President John F. Kennedy once said, "The problems of this world cannot possibly be solved by skeptics or cynics, whose horizons are limited by the obvious realities. We need men who can dream of things that never were, and ask, 'Why not?'"

I think the answer to "Why not?" is found in faith. It's faith that calls people to step out: "Faith is the assurance of things hoped for, the conviction of things not seen" (Heb. 11:1). If your vision doesn't require faith, it's not going to change anything—including you. Vision is thinking about the impossible and believing God will enable you to see it through. Jesus said, "If you have faith the size of a mustard seed, you will say to this mountain, 'Move from here to there,' and it will move; and nothing will be impossible to you" (Matt. 17:20). His point is not for us to change the topography of the earth, but to trust that, with faith, we can overcome the "mountains" or seemingly impossible obstacles in our life journey. Your destiny is there, just beyond that mountain. When God gives us a vision and faith for the impossible, nothing is impossible! Through faith, we can stare impossibilities in the face and ask, "Why not?"

Step 2: Share the Future

When you think you've identified your vision, the next step is to share it with others. Why? Because going public will make it that much more real. Just be wise in deciding who you share it with first. Do you remember the Old Testament story about Joseph? He wasn't exactly being wise when he told his older brothers he'd dreamed that they would one day bow down to him. His brothers were so angry and offended, they nearly killed him before deciding instead to sell him into slavery.

I can't tell you how many times I made the mistake of sharing my vision with the wrong people. Like Joseph, I naively thought people would celebrate when I had a positive vision. I thought they'd do that because I knew I would do that for them. The Bible says, "To the pure, all things are pure; but to those who are defiled and unbelieving, nothing is pure" (Titus 1:15). This means that people with pure hearts think everyone has a pure heart, but people with corrupt hearts think everyone has a corrupt heart. Your vision may bring out things in people's hearts you never knew were there. More likely than not, people without a vision of their own will misunderstand your vision. So seek out people who won't be threatened or intimidated by your vision and who will be willing to celebrate it with you.

When you share your vision with the right people, you increase your chances of achieving it. By articulating it, you clarify it. By making it public, you deepen your commitment to it and build the momentum needed to carry it out. Perhaps most importantly, sharing your vision with people who know you and know God gives you a chance to refine or redirect your vision. They may see a flaw in your approach or even your destination. On the other hand, if they give you a thumbs-up, you can move forward toward your destiny with greater confidence.

Feedback from trusted family members, friends, and colleagues will especially help you to verify two things—your motives and whether your vision is God-given.

Verify Your Motives

As you share your vision, check and recheck your motives with people you trust. Remember, God's vision is accomplished through us, not focused on us. Ask yourself and others:

- Is this a God-honoring vision?
- Will my efforts to achieve it harm anyone?
- Who besides me might it benefit?

Of course, *you* will benefit from your vision, but if your vision is from God, others will benefit as well. Make sure God's purpose drives your vision. I see people all the time who come up with their own vision and then try to slap God's name on it. Walt Kallestad, author of *Wake Up Your Dreams*, calls these people "schemers," as opposed to "dreamers."[2] Consider the difference between schemers and dreamers, and ask yourself which category you fall into. This is a key step in verifying your motives.

SCHEMERS	DREAMERS
Emphasize profits	Emphasize people
Goal = success	Goal = significance
Self-given vision	God-given vision
Corrupt the world	Build the world
Ask: What can I get?	Ask: What can I give?

As competitors, schemers count every battle. They are constantly looking at the outcome of today. It's all about how they appeared, how much they profited, and who applauded them. Their vision is focused on themselves. Dreamers, on the other hand, are constantly looking toward the horizon. Their vision is unlimited because they are building significance for tomorrow.

Verify your motives. Again, whose vision are you fulfilling? If your vision does not achieve God's purpose, it will make only a temporal difference. The wisdom of Scripture is clear: "Many are the plans in a person's heart, but it is the LORD's purpose that prevails" (Prov. 19:21 NIV).

Verify That Your Vision Is God-Given

As you share your future with others, ask them to help you verify that your vision is God-given. There are three qualities of a God-given vision you need to look for.

1. *A God-given vision is always beyond your ability.* If you don't have to leave your comfort zone to achieve your vision, there is a pretty good chance it's not from God. Why would God give you a vision for something already within your reach? He wants us to stretch and grow! Why else would He call a man like Moses, who had a speech impediment, to lead the nation of Israel out of slavery in Egypt? Or why would He call a

timid man like Gideon to be a mighty warrior and defeat the Midianite army? I think you get the idea.

You don't have to have great talent to accomplish God's calling, just great vision. The woman we remember as Mother Teresa didn't strike anyone who knew her in her early life as being anything but ordinary. Her colleagues from the convent indicated she wasn't an extraordinary student and was never much of a leader. But God broke her heart with a vision for the poor and vulnerable of India. It was this undeniable vision that enabled her to overcome her limitations and impact not just one nation, but the world. Skills are a poor substitute for vision.

Perhaps God has given you a vision to help vulnerable children and families overseas, yet the very idea overwhelms you. A trusted friend may be able to help you see the hidden abilities or resources that would enable you to fulfill this vision. What at first seems impossible may actually be more possible than you realize.

2. *A God-given vision gives you peace.* I have made many mistakes and had a lifetime of struggles, but I have never once lost the peace in my heart that I am doing what God called me to do. If it had been merely a vision of my own creation, I never would have seen it through. Instead, I find joy even in the problems and the sacrifices because I have the confidence of knowing that God is working out His vision through me.

When you share your vision with others, also share the impact it has on your heart. Does talking about it leave you feeling excited despite the obstacles? Does it bring you a sense of peace as you draw closer to God? Invite the people you trust to comment on what they observe in you when you discuss and work toward your vision. Their insights may resolve any lingering doubts.

3. *A God-given vision shows signs of God's blessing.* God not only initiates the vision; He also ensures the vision and also provides the resources for His vision. When I accepted the offer to become pastor at Cascade Hills, the church was in debt, the offerings were next to nothing,

and thirty-two wonderful but discouraged people were struggling to keep the doors open. I had no experience and they had no money, but we knew God had put us together. One of our first confirmations of God's vision came as the little church began to grow.

In prayer one morning, I sensed that we were supposed to begin a building program to enable us to reach more people. I walked into the secretary's office and said, "I believe God is going to provide financially for a building program." Deloris laughed and commented on the state of our offerings, which averaged less than three hundred dollars a week. "It will take a lot more than what we have," she said. I agreed.

Later that day, I conducted the funeral of a sixteen-year-old boy named Stevie Mobley. He was a great kid with good looks and personality who'd been raised by his aunt and uncle. He'd lost his life in a tragic car accident. After the funeral, his uncle approached me. "Bill," he said, "I am so glad that you are reaching young people for God. I want to give you a gift to start a building program to reach more young people like Stevie." I thanked him and put the folded check he handed me into my pocket without looking at it. When I returned to the office, I handed the folded check to Deloris and said, "I just got the first check for a building program." She opened it, looked at me with wide eyes, and said, "I guess you can get it started with ten thousand dollars!"

I was floored. For a little church with nothing, this was huge. When Sunday came, I shared the story with the people in church. Suddenly, a lady on our finance committee stood up and started walking down the aisle. When she reached the front, she slipped off her wedding ring and handed it to me. "Pastor," she said, "this is a ring from a man I loved. He left me this ring before he died. Last Sunday, as I sat cramped in this crowded little church, I felt God was telling me to give you this ring to sell and begin a building program. I wrestled with God about that. I knew what I was supposed to do, but I bargained with God. I told God that I would be glad to give this ring as a contribution once we already had ten thousand dollars collected." She said she knew how bad the church finances were, so she thought it would be at least two or three years before she would have to act. Now, just one week later, we had the ten thousand dollars. The woman handed me the ring and the church celebrated.

I knew very little about the value of diamond rings. When Debbie and I got married, I gave her a "Jesus" diamond—it was so small only Jesus could see it. It cost me eighty-eight dollars. Now I had a much larger ring, which I carried around in my pocket for days. Every time I met someone, I showed it off. I even let several women try it on. I held it up to the light to look at all the beams of colored light shooting around the room.

Wednesday of that week, I went into a Baskin-Robbins ice-cream shop and noticed a jewelry store next door. I took in the ring, asked for a quick appraisal, and returned after eating ice cream next door. When I walked in, the jeweler said, "Bill, where did you get this ring?" I explained what had happened in church the weekend before.

"No, really," he said. "How did you get this ring?" I told him again.

"This ring," he said, "is worth thirty-seven thousand five hundred dollars." I was stunned. When I told the people in church on Sunday, the whole place broke loose. People started donating antiques, jewelry, valuables, property, and more. God was confirming His vision.

When I shared my vision about the building program with my secretary, and later with my congregation, God blessed it beyond anything I'd imagined. In a sense, by voicing my vision, I invited God to show me whether that vision really did come from Him. The results removed any doubt for me or for our church.

You can do the same. Let the people you trust know when you feel you've received a vision from God; then wait to see what happens. Talk it over with those people. If God blesses you or your trusted advisers in a way that advances your vision, you'll know you're on the right track.

Step 3: Plan the Future

A dream and a vision are like two kinds of light. Your dream is like the light of a lightbulb—it casts a soft glow that helps you find what you're looking for. Your vision is more like the intense and focused light of a laser beam—it has the power to cut and shape anything in its path. In order for your dream to take on the focused, laser-like power of true vision, it must be channeled into a plan of action.

If you ask most people where they're going in life or what their plans are, they'll probably be able to tell you what they have planned for the weekend but not much else. In fact, studies have shown that the average person spends more time planning a vacation than planning a strategy to achieve his or her destiny. Baseball's Yogi Berra used to say, "If you don't know where you are going, you might wind up someplace else."

When it comes to channeling vision into a plan of action, we need to think long-term. I have a friend named Mrs. Mitchell who understands this principle. She is ninety-nine years old, with a keen mind and a lot of energy. Conversations with her always leave me feeling I have a long way to go and a lot yet to learn in life. She recently described to me her ten-year life plan. Ten years! And she's ninety-nine now! She's making plans to write a book, meet country singer George Strait (in case you're reading, George, she'd make your day), and travel abroad. I know people who are thirty who don't have a life plan, but Mrs. Mitchell is still planning everything except her funeral. When we focus on the long term, we're better able to plot a clear course to achieve our vision.

My focused, driving vision is to use my role as a pastor to love and relate to people, especially those who don't yet know God. I try to measure and filter everything I do through that lens. Dabbling in other activities wastes my energy and frustrates other people because I'm in their way. I can't get off at every distracting exit ramp I see on the highway of my life and still hope to achieve my vision.

If you want something badly enough, you'll make a plan and find a way to do it. That's what a would-be novelist named Kathryn Stockett did. Her dream was to write a novel that would "draw a picture of a certain time and place"—white households with black housekeepers in the 1960s South. When she first started writing, Kathryn didn't truly believe anyone would read her work. But as she wrote and developed her characters, her dream solidified into a vision. This was a story that had to be published.

Kathryn spent eighteen months writing and polishing a manuscript and then mailed it to a literary agent. Six weeks later, she received a rejection letter. Instead of getting discouraged, Kathryn went back to editing. Her plan was to keep at it, using the advice of agents to make her manuscript better. Months later, she sent the revised manuscript to several more literary agents. This time she received fifteen rejections. "Maybe the next book will be the one that gets you published," a friend said. But Kathryn still believed in her vision. A year and a half later, Kathryn opened her fortieth rejection letter, which read, "There is no market for this kind of tired writing." That was a tough weekend for Kathryn. She cried. But she stuck to her plan.

After five years of writing and rewriting, Kathryn had accumulated sixty rejection letters. The sixty-first letter, however, was from an agent named Susan Ramer. She wanted to represent Kathryn. Three weeks later, Ramer sold *The Help* to Amy Einhorn Books. It was published in 2009, spent more than one hundred weeks on the *New York Times* best-seller list, sold five million copies within two years, and was made into a movie.[3] Kathryn's unrelenting vision and commitment to following her plan led to her success.

When you build a vision, the vision also builds you. It becomes a filter to help you determine what to do and what not to do. At times, you'll have to say no to good things because they don't line up with your vision. For example, whenever we consider starting a new ministry at Cascade Hills, the first thing I do with my staff is filter it through our vision, which is to bring the message of Christ to people who don't yet know Him. If the new ministry doesn't help us achieve that vision, we don't do it. We have had to say no to many good ideas in order to stick to our vision. Launching programs that don't build, enhance, or better achieve the vision will inevitably detract from it and derail us in the long run. You've got to learn to say no to the good in order to accomplish the best in your life.

Tom Monaghan was committed to his vision. Although he was an orphan of a poor family in Michigan, he envisioned one day owning the Detroit Tigers. Today, he is known as the founder of Domino's Pizza, the pizza delivery company with annual sales exceeding $2 billion. And in 1983, he paid $53 million for the Tigers. When asked how he fulfilled his dream, he replied, "When the opportunity came, I was ready for it. A lot of people around me would see me doing things that made no sense to them at all, but I had a big jump on them. I was thinking about these things years ago."[4]

Tom knew what he wanted to accomplish, made a plan, and focused all his efforts on getting there. When he did, people thought he got lucky, but Tom knew he had spent years following a precise plan for how he was going to achieve the vision.

If God has given you a vision, you need a plan that details the steps that will get you there. Maybe your vision is to one day start a recording studio in your town. It won't just "happen." Your long-term plan will likely include a year or two of connecting with musicians, finding a location, purchasing the right equipment, and coming up with a marketing plan. You'll want to go to any and every venue where music is happening to get your name out there and attract new talent. Your plan might also include interviewing people who already run successful recording studios. The details and timeline may change as you go, but having a plan is essential.

Visions are realized when you invest your time and energy in a long-term plan. If you find yourself getting frustrated waiting for your vision to become a reality, continue to focus on and refine the plan. If you keep working toward your vision, you'll be ready for your opportunity when it comes.

Step 4: Create the Future

In 1993, Troy and Kim Meeder decided to purchase some property in central Oregon and start a small ranch. The only land they could afford was a nine-acre rock quarry, which had been used to mine cinders for spreading on area roads during the winter months. The land was devastated—no trees, no grass, not even topsoil. But the Meeders had a vision that this land could be turned into a working ranch—and maybe that it could become even more.

Troy and Kim began collecting and spreading organic waste materials from neighboring ranches to rehabilitate their land. They planted scraggly trees that no one else wanted. Gradually, the barren property came back to life. Kim even acquired a pair of broken-down horses. One was malnourished and near death, and the other had been severely beaten by its former owner. The Meeders invited children to visit the ranch and to spend time with and help care for the horses. When one of those kids, a young girl believed to be mute, began talking to one of the horses, Troy and Kim suddenly grasped the vision God had for their land and their lives. In 1995, they founded Crystal Peaks Youth Ranch. Today, the ranch is a home for neglected and abused horses, and every year those horses interact with more than four thousand visitors, many of whom are disadvantaged or abused children in need of a horse's healing touch.[5]

It took years of hard work for Troy and Kim Meeder to turn Crystal Peaks Youth Ranch from a dream into reality. And it didn't just happen—with God's help, they *created* their future. You can create your future in the same way. Although your future belongs to God, He entrusts it to you as you take steps of faith and commit to carrying out His vision for you.

Most people operate from the perspective of either their past, their present circumstances, or their emotions. You can choose instead to operate from your future. When God gives you a vision, He's giving you a glimpse of what He has planned for your future. Don't let the future just happen to you—join with God and create it. Commit to do it step by step, and to do it in spite of the obstacles you face.

Do It Step by Step

Your vision may not come to pass all at once, but don't get discouraged. Seeing your vision become reality is like running a marathon. You finish by completing one step and one mile at a time. God's vision for your life is a marathon, not a hundred-meter dash, so you have to pace yourself.

Sara Blakely is one of the wealthiest and most influential women in the world, but she didn't achieve success overnight. Her vision was to create footless and more comfortable pantyhose for women. While working in sales at an office supply company in Florida, she tested and developed her product. She bought a textbook on patents and applied for one. Finally, she took a week off of work to present her idea to hosiery manufacturers in North Carolina. All turned her down—but one later called back, saying that his daughters supported her idea.

After another year spent developing a prototype, she met with a Neiman Marcus product buyer in Dallas, personally showing off her new hosiery, now called Spanx, in the ladies' room. The buyer agreed to put Spanx on Neiman Marcus shelves. Sara spent the following year visiting stores and introducing her product to customers. She also sent her product to Oprah Winfrey's television show. When Oprah named Sara's pantyhose as a "favorite product," Sara was on her way. Today she is a billionaire and was recently named by *Forbes* magazine as one of the one hundred most powerful women in the world.[6]

Sara's focus on her vision allowed her to patiently and consistently take the steps necessary to achieve it. The same can be true for your vision. Take it one step at a time.

Do It in Spite of the Obstacles

While God's vision is perfect, not every day and every experience in the process of achieving that vision will be. Expect obstacles; the road to the next level is always uphill. The great thing about obstacles is that they can accelerate your growth if you let them. Keep pressing forward. Chances are good that the seed of your next opportunity is hidden within your greatest setback.

Drew Wills understands this. In 2004, Drew was paralyzed from the waist down in a skiing accident in Aspen, Colorado. Those first few days in a rehabilitation center were grim. He'd been an avid cyclist before the accident and assumed that those days were over. But things began to change when he learned about handcycles and other adaptive outdoor equipment. Suddenly, he had a whole new vision for his future. Which is why, just a little more than a year after his accident, he partici-pated in the 2005 Bicycle Tour of Colorado, a weeklong journey through the Rocky Mountains. Earlier in the week, brutal weather and fatigue twice forced him to drop out ahead of the finish line. On this leg, a 110-mile day trek, he feared he wasn't going to make it again.

Despite the sweat on his back and exhaustion in his arms, however, Drew pushed on. The miles rolled by. When he reached the end of a long downhill stretch and entered a valley that opened into scrub oak and grassy fields of the desert and plains, his outlook began to change. *You know,* he thought, *I just might be able to do this.*

Fifteen miles from the finish line, Drew was sure of it. He would finish the race. *If I can do this, there are all kinds of things I can do.*

And there were. In 2007, Drew placed second at the Off-Road Handcycling World Championships. In 2009, he won the event. Also that year, he was the second American finisher among long-seat riders in the Sadler's Alaska Challenge, the longest and toughest handcycle race on the planet. He eventually returned to full-time work as an attorney, trying cases in the courtroom, serving on local nonprofit boards, and providing for his family. He also regained his enjoyment of Colorado's slopes on a monoski and celebrated his twenty-fifth wedding anniversary by earning open water certification, then scuba diving with his wife in the Caribbean.[7]

As Drew Wills discovered, vision enables you to go beyond the obstacles you assumed were insurmountable. When the apostle Paul said, "I press on toward the goal for the prize of the upward call of God in Christ Jesus" (Phil. 3:14), he was describing his persistent, tenacious commitment to God's vision for his life. The Greek word for the phrase "press on" is *dioko*. To better understand the meaning, picture an athlete in a footrace, arms and legs outstretched, muscles taut, straining to cross a finish line. It's that point in the race when athletes are giving it all they've got even though they might feel like there's nothing left to give. It's at this point in the race toward your dreams that you have to press on—lean into God's vision and allow it to draw you, strengthen you, and motivate you to overcome the obstacles you encounter. Woodrow Wilson said that a man who has hope that his dream will come true should nourish, protect, and nurse it through the bad days to live it out later. We have more than hope in our dreams. We have unshakable confidence to live out God's vision for our lives, even in the face of obstacles.

Step 5: Risk the Future

Some people make progress toward their vision and then trade it for security. The risk of continual growth becomes too great when they look around and see all they've accumulated and fear they could lose it. As their fear of loss increases, they opt to play it safe. Like a football team that shifts into "prevent defense" and plays not to lose rather than to win, the very thing they try to avoid is often what they soon create.

It's been said that the safest place you could ever be is in the center of God's will. In fact, there is no security in this life except when we are living out God's vision for our lives. I love the statement Helen Keller used to make: "Why play life safe? None of us are getting out of it alive anyway."

The greatest enemy of tomorrow's success is today's success. Many growing people become stagnant when they reach a few goals and become comfortable with just getting by. Oliver Wendell Holmes observed, "I find the great thing in this world is not so much where we stand as in what direction we are moving." You have to keep vision in front of you to keep moving forward.

How do you know if you've lost your will to risk? One sure sign is that you're overly focused on protecting what you have. There's nothing wrong with buying life insurance or building up a nice retirement fund, but how much do you really need? You can't take it with you, but you *can* put it to use to achieve your vision. Another sign that you've stopped risking and growing is worrying about what people think. Was Jesus concerned about the opinion of the Pharisees? Should you base your actions on the opinions of acquaintances who know nothing about the vision God has etched on your heart? God wants you to listen to Him, not to your neighbors.

If you wake up each day feeling that you've "arrived" and that there are no new challenges ahead, it may mean that you've stopped short of fulfilling the complete vision God has for you. Taking chances for God is what a life of faith is all about! Jesus put it this way: "Risk your life and get more than you ever dreamed of. Play it safe and end up holding the bag" (Luke 19:26 MSG).

Seeing Through the Fog

Do you have an idea of how to envision your God-designed future and how to get there? I hope so. It's never too late to put aside the life you've been living and step into your destiny. As ninety-nine-year-old Mrs. Mitchell demonstrates, age is no limit. Abraham was one hundred years old when God started his lineage as the father of Israel. Sarah was ninety when God told her she would have a child. Moses was eighty before God called him to lead the Israelites out of Egypt. Caleb charged his mountain in the Promised Land after his eighties.

You still have time to accomplish your goals and reach for your dreams. In fact, when you die, you should still be reaching for your vision. Vision should outlast the visionary. If you pursue dreams that will live on after you, they won't cease to exist at the end of your earthly life. In the 1960s, Truett Cathy founded the Chick-fil-A restaurant chain, which is known as much for its corporate culture as for its popular chicken sandwiches. Truett Cathy's vision included establishing a business in which people could honor God by not working on Sundays or Christmas. Though Truett died in 2014, his vision for Chick-fil-A lives on. God's vision for your life is not necessarily limited to your life. You can fulfill all that He has planned for you and impact the world for generations as long as you have the courage to fix that vision in your mind and never waver from your course.

In 1952, Florence Chadwick attempted to become the first woman to swim across California's Catalina Channel. On the morning of her first attempt, the water was bone-chillingly cold and the fog was so dense she could hardly see the boats following her. After nearly sixteen hours and only a few hundred feet from land, she gave up—not because of the fatigue or the cold, but because of the fog. She told a reporter, "Look, I'm not excusing myself, but if I could have seen land I know I could have made it." The fog alone defeated her because it obscured her vision.

Two months later, she swam that same channel, and again the fog obscured her view, but this time she swam with faith as her vision. She could "see" the land in her mind when she could not see it with her eyes. This time Florence Chadwick finished and beat the men's record for the swim by two hours.[8]

My prayer is that you will let the vision God has given you lead the way into your future. Where will you be if you don't?

Insights for Inspiration

- The best way to achieve a dream is to aim beyond it.
- Vision becomes a filter to help you determine what to do and what not to do.
- People without a vision of their own will likely misunderstand yours.
- You can choose to operate from the perspective of your future.
- Vision should be out of reach but not out of sight.

Verse to Review

"For the vision is yet for the appointed time; it hastens toward the goal and it will not fail. Though it tarries, wait for it; for it will certainly come, it will not delay" (Hab. 2:3).

Getting Personal

- Which would you say has the most influence on how you make your important decisions—your past, your present, or your vision for the future?
- Have you shared your vision with others? Why or why not?
- How do you feel about beginning to actively pursue your vision? Scared? Excited? Overwhelmed?
- Do you feel it's too late to achieve your dreams? If so, why?

Faith over Fear

To dare is to lose one's footing momentarily.
To not dare is to lose oneself.
Søren Kierkegaard

Did you know you have a risk style? You might be *risk-avoidant*, doing everything you can to eliminate any potential negative outcome. Or you could be just the opposite, which is *risk-seeking*, always looking to live on the thrilling edge of danger. If it depends on the situation, you might be *risk-neutral*, choosing to either avoid or seek risk in different circumstances. Generally speaking, most of us prefer to avoid risk when we can. We buckle our seatbelts. We insure our vacations. We buy extended warranties for big purchases. We sign up for the best medical insurance we can afford. We draw up prenuptial agreements. Why take a pointless risk on such things?

Minimizing risk is often the wisest and best course of action, but sometimes risk aversion can prevent us from taking legitimate and healthy risks, especially when the risks are in pursuit of our goals and dreams. We've come to believe that if we take a risk and fall short, we've suffered an unforgivable failure. We don't move on to a new city or new job because we fear it won't work out. We don't sign up for that auto shop or theater or exercise class because we're afraid of how we'll look in the eyes of others if we don't do well. If this tendency continues unchecked, we might come to believe that taking risks is neither desirable nor necessary. And we couldn't be more wrong.

A willingness to take God-honoring risks is fundamental to growth and success. It is, in fact, one of God's gifts to us—a gift that enables us to break free of obstacles and limitations so we can discover and live into our destiny.

Risk offers multiple benefits to the risk-taker. The coffee giant Starbucks, for example, is known as one of the most innovative and profitable companies in the world. It is quick to introduce new products and digital enhancements, even if the product or enhancement still has some rough edges. This risky strategy has paid off more often than not. "We do not want to sit on our hands," says Adam Brotman, the firm's chief digital officer. "If we feel excited about something, we'll get it out there, learn our lessons, and correct the mistakes. It's not always the most stress-free way to launch, but it's the fastest."[1]

On a personal level, risk can be just as beneficial. Gwen Alexander, a woman in our church, knows just how rewarding taking a personal risk can be. Several years ago, she approached me after church one Sunday and said, "Pastor, I've always wanted to go to college, but I've been afraid to try. No one in my family has ever gone to college."

I encouraged her to go. "But that's four years," she said. Gwen was twenty-seven at the time and afraid she was too old to go back to school.

"If you go back to school now, how old will you be when you graduate in four years?" I asked.

"Thirty-one," she said.

"And how old will you be in four years if you don't go back to school?" I asked.

She smiled.

"You'll be the same age!" I said. "You should go!"

Two years later, Gwen sent me an invitation to her associate's degree graduation ceremony. I sent her a gift and a note of congratulations that said, "I knew you could do it!" Two years after that, I received another graduation announcement—she'd earned her bachelor's degree. Even that wasn't the end of it. Two years after that, I received yet another invitation, this time for her master's degree graduation ceremony. And that was followed a few years later by an invitation to the ceremony for her doctoral degree. Gwen then took a position as a school principal and loves her new career as a professional educator. It was possible only because she risked breaking out of her comfort zone and reaching for her dream.

Taking healthy risks is a good strategy for more than corporations and careers. It's a key to intimate and thriving relationships. For example, when a normally silent husband opens up to his wife about mistakes he's made at work or his concerns about their marriage, it creates a sense of bonding and trust. When a wife is willing to cheerfully join her husband in activities she may not necessarily love, it fosters a sense of partnership. Both steps require risk because they could lead to ridicule. The husband or wife who makes that first move is left in a vulnerable position. But the rewards almost always far outweigh the risks.

Risk is also important in building up our confidence and a healthy self-image. One of the best ways to increase confidence is to take a risk. Why? Because in order to grow, you have to get some "wins" under your belt—and you can't get a win without risking a loss. When my kids were younger, I coached their baseball teams. One of the players on our team had a difficult home life that had damaged his self-esteem. All season long, he never swung at a single pitch. Whenever he was up to bat, he was too terrified of striking out to swing. Finally, in the last game, I pulled him aside and said, "No matter what happens when you get up to bat, just swing at the ball. I don't care if you strike out, just swing!"

During his next at-bat, he got up and swung for the first time. *Crack!* The ball went right between third base and shortstop. He was so excited, he ran like a rabbit and ended up scoring an inside-the-park home run on that first swing! Had he chosen not to swing, he would have taken another defeated walk back to the dugout. But not this time. It was his *attempt* at success that enabled him to experience success.

At the start of the next season, with a smile on his face, he said to me in front of his friends, "Do you remember that home run I got in the last game of the season?"

"I sure do," I said. "You changed the game!" I couldn't help noticing what a different boy he was simply because he had taken the risk to swing.

Of all the benefits of risk, however, perhaps the most important is how risk increases our faith. God created us to take risks that will benefit us physically, intellectually, and emotionally. So it only makes sense that He created us to risk in ways that also benefit us spiritually. In fact, virtually every good thing He offers must begin with our willingness to risk: belief, trust, love. Jesus calls us to risk again and again: "Anyone who chooses to do the will of God will find out whether my teaching comes from God or whether I speak on my own" (John 7:17 NIV); "If you abide in Me, and My words abide in you, ask whatever you wish, and it will be done for you" (John 15:7). You can almost hear Jesus saying, "Go ahead, ask—I dare you!"

When God gave us free will—the ability to choose or reject Him—He risked His love on us. When Jesus died on the cross, He risked His life on the hope that we would choose to believe in Him and follow Him. Risk is what takes us deeper into the life of faith and closer to our God-designed destiny. In fact, it's the only way to discover the plan God has for each of us, which makes it an adventure all its own.

Author and former investigative reporter Lee Strobel puts it this way:

> When we take a risk, we're stretching beyond what we think are our limits in order to reach for a goal. Inevitably, that involves overcoming some sort of fear—fear of the unknown, of physical harm, of failure, of humiliation, even of success. And it involves adventure.
>
> When I was in college a friend often lent me his Kawasaki motorcycle, which was primarily designed for off-road use. When

I'd ride thirty miles an hour down the smooth residential streets toward campus, it was safe but boring. Wind whipped my hair but my heart didn't quiver. However, when I'd go zipping off the road, through tall weeds, down twisting dirt trails, dodging trees and bushes, around boulders, and up steep inclines—places where I was facing some risk—that was exciting.

The same could be said for living a life of faith. It's when we overcome our fears and take spiritual risks that we really experience the adventure of Christianity. Jesus said, in effect, that those who risk their whole life will find it, but those who hang on to their life—those who shrink back from risk—will be the losers.[2]

So what's your risk style going to be when it comes to pursuing your destiny? Are you willing to be risk-seeking, to follow God into your future? If you're still feeling a little risk-averse, let's talk about some of the things that might be holding you back—and what you can do about them.

Risk-Takers, Caretakers, and Undertakers

Risk requires the courage to move forward when the outcome is uncertain. You're always moving in a direction—either forward or backward—so taking risks is the best option to help you keep moving forward. It's just like riding a bicycle—if you stop exerting the effort to move forward, you'll fall. Sure, you might be able to keep some forward motion going by coasting, but you can only coast when you're going downhill. At some point, you'll still lose your momentum.

I've found that when it comes to taking risks and moving forward, people tend to fall into one of three categories: undertakers, caretakers, and risk-takers. Undertakers are definitely not in the process of moving forward. Because their best victories and growth are all in the past, they put their energies into trying to maintain the glow of previous accomplishments. They have no dreams or goals to work toward.

Caretakers are all about the present. They don't rely on past growth and accomplishments, but they don't take action to move forward either. Instead, they hold on tight right where they are and put their best energies into protecting what they have. They've fallen into the trap of self-protection and are unwilling to risk loss or vulnerability. But they won't remain caretakers for long. Soon their lack of forward motion will cause them to slip into the undertaker category.

Risk-takers, on the other hand, learn from the past, live in the present, and focus on the future. They are consistently in forward motion. They may stumble at times, but they are alive with hope and never stop making adjustments and trying again.

We choose to live in one of these three categories. We do it through our attitudes and actions. The history of football illustrates what happens when we choose between maintenance or protection and risk. Football began as a running game. When the forward pass was first introduced to the sport, many players thought it was a dumb idea. In the first professional game where the forward pass was allowed, only one team used it. They were the risk-takers. The other team maintained a running game. These players were caretakers. What do you think happened? The risk-takers won, 109–6. While holding on to their regular, comfortable game, the caretakers were demoted to undertakers. They got slaughtered!

Remember our discussion of the crab from chapter 2? When the crab sheds its old shell, it takes a huge risk that leaves it vulnerable to predators. But the process of molting also rids the crab of parasites and barnacles that have attached themselves to the old shell. At each new level of growth, chances are good that you'll be divinely separated from whatever it is that once held you back. This could take the form of anything from shedding "parasitic" people to overcoming self-defeating behaviors and thought patterns. Whatever the case, such "tearing away" is a natural part of the growth process. Remember, a crab that doesn't shed its old shell will die. Likewise, when we quit taking risks—when we become caretakers or undertakers—our dreams and potential start to die.

Fear of Failure

So what prevents us from taking God-honoring and beneficial risks? More often than not, it's fear of failure. People who never realize their dreams tend to view failure as "the end." They take it personally when something doesn't work out. They think, "If *it* failed, *I'm* a failure." Their identity is tied to the success or failure of their efforts.

I'm sure you've heard the saying, "Success went to their heads." But I've also met many people for whom the opposite is true—failure went to their heads. Comedian Ron White has said that one time his grandfather looked at him and then said to his father, "Now that boy's got a whole lot of quit in him." That's not really a trait you want to master. You've heard it said, "Quitting is not an option," but that's not true. Quitting is always an option. And many of us routinely choose it because failure feels too painful to repeat.

It's only natural to behave in self-protective ways after we experience a setback. To avoid pain, we revert to what's comfortable and allow that to become the dominant factor in our decision making. It doesn't matter if this means living a life that falls short of our desires and dreams. We'll continue to do what's "safe" as long as we don't have to experience the pain of another failure. This means we'll end up exactly where we've always been. We fail to succeed, not because we fail, but because we fear failure.

People who succeed have a different perspective on failure. They may not like it, but they understand that there is a certain amount woven into the fabric of success. Those who work in sales know this well. Did you know that, on average, a salesperson is rejected eleven times before making one sale? I once heard about a salesman complaining to his boss about the rejections he'd encountered. Discouraged, he told his boss he'd been rejected six times. Without any sympathy his boss replied, "Good! You're getting closer. Only five more tries till you make the sale." That's the same kind of perspective we need to bring to our own setbacks and failures.

Successful people aren't necessarily smarter; they just keep getting up one more time. Inventor James Dyson had an idea for keeping the suction in vacuum cleaners strong as they picked up dirt, but he went through more than five thousand prototypes before finding a model that worked. Movie director Steven Spielberg had his application rejected three times by the University of Southern California School of Theater, Film and Television. Evan Williams founded a podcasting platform called Odeo that quickly became obsolete before he cofounded the social media service Twitter. Richard Branson had dyslexia and a poor academic record before becoming a billionaire businessman and investor. Tenacity in the face of failure is part of almost every successful person's journey. Those who try and fail are always better off than those who never try. Besides, you never really fail until you quit trying.

Here's a definition of fear that I've found helpful. It's an acrostic:

False
Evidence
Appearing
Real

Fear may be an emotion, but it's also a way of thinking. And when you let false evidence dictate your choices, you're thinking irrationally. Remember the story of Chicken Little? An excitable chicken gets hit in the head with an acorn and starts spreading false "evidence." Convinced it's not an acorn but a piece of the sky that has landed on her head, she runs around like a crazy bird telling everyone the sky is falling. All the animals panic because they consider her false evidence to be fact. She's clearly terrified, so it must be true! The fox is the only one wise enough to think rationally and check out the evidence for himself. When his investigation reveals that the sky is in fact *not* falling, he leads all the animals into the "safety" of his den where he intends to make a meal out of them.

Chicken Little and her friends suffer more from their fear of the problem than from the problem itself. And it's their fear that ultimately leads them into real danger. False evidence keeps them from thinking rationally, and they follow the fox right into his den.

When you allow fear to dominate your thinking and decision making, you're actually moving toward danger rather than away from it. Consider the impact of fear:

- *Fear destroys your dreams.* Fear keeps us from focusing on the future. It uses false evidence to distract you from reaching your dreams.

- *Fear paralyzes you.* You no longer have the confidence you need to take action and keep moving forward.

- *Fear directs your destiny.* Your decisions and actions are limited to overly self-protective choices. Unable to take legitimate risks, you lose the ability to live into your destiny.

The disciple Peter gives us a picture of what happens when fear dominates our decision making. One night while Peter and the other disciples were in a boat, Jesus came to them by walking on the water. Peter said, "Lord, if it is You, command me to come to You on the water" (Matt. 14:28). When Jesus invited him to come, Peter got out of the boat and started walking toward Jesus on the water. Suddenly, however, Peter's focus shifted from Jesus to the wind and waves around him. Remember, what you focus on, you feel—and what Peter felt was fear. It paralyzed him. He began to sink until he cried out for help and Jesus rescued him.

One minute, Peter stepped out in faith in pursuit of his destiny and was standing on the water with Jesus. The next minute, he was focused on fear and sinking like a rock. When his focus changed, his circumstances changed.

Do you sometimes allow fear to drive your decisions? It doesn't have to be that way. Tenacity and a focus on God's future for you will enable you to overcome your fears. As we're about to see, it's a matter of perspective.

Glancing and Gazing

When my son B.J. was a little boy, I took him to the doctor for his first shot. When we came out of the doctor's office, I said, "Son, I'm proud of you. You didn't cry."

He looked up at me innocently and asked, "Was I supposed to?"

I laughed—we had forgotten to tell him it might hurt! Since no one informed him that he should be afraid, he wasn't. He went in with a positive perspective and ended up with a positive experience.

When I encourage you to adjust your perspective on risk and failure, I'm not suggesting that you ignore your problems or pretend they don't exist. Perspective is simply a point of view that makes some things look smaller and other things look bigger. I love how the Old Testament story of Joshua and Caleb demonstrates the dramatic difference it makes to have the right perspective.

After God's people were freed from slavery in Egypt, they were finally ready to conquer the Promised Land. Joshua and Caleb were among the advance team sent out by Moses to assess both the land and the strengths and weaknesses of the people in it. But the team brought back a mixed report. While the land was indeed flowing with milk and honey, the people who lived there were described as powerful and living in fortified cities (Num. 13:27–28). When Caleb said they could certainly take possession of the land, this was the response of the other men on the advance team:

> "We can't attack those people; they are stronger than we are." And they spread among the Israelites a bad report about the land they had explored. They said, "The land we explored devours those living in it. All the people we saw there are of great size. . . . We seemed like grasshoppers in our own eyes, and we looked the same to them." (Numbers 13:31–33 NIV)

Did you catch the whopping perspective shift in that passage—not to mention the false evidence that got spread around? When their fears overruled their faith, the men were reduced to grasshoppers "in their own eyes." In other words, it was their perspective that made them feel small and weak. In contrast, Caleb's perspective was focused on God— God was certainly bigger and more powerful than the giants. Both Caleb and Joshua had faith that the same God who had rescued them from slavery would give them victory over the giants. Faith overruled their fears because they only *glanced* at the problem but *gazed* at the Problem-Solver.

It's only human to experience fear in the face of a threat, but even when we have legitimate reasons to be afraid, we can still choose our perspective—what we glance at gets smaller, while what we gaze at gets bigger. Focusing our gaze on God makes both God and our faith bigger. In the human heart, fear and faith are opposites fighting for dominance—one will always try to crowd out the other. The one you focus on and feed is the one that grows. Trusting God grows our faith and suppresses fear. You can rely on this promise: "God hath not given us the spirit of fear; but of power, and of love, and of a sound mind" (2 Tim. 1:7 KJV).

I once read a story about a man who tried an experiment with fleas. He put fleas in a bottle with a lid on top. At first the fleas tried to jump out, but they kept hitting their heads on the lid. They quickly learned how high they could jump without hitting the lid. Later, when the lid was taken off, they still didn't jump out of the bottle because they were afraid of the pain of hitting the lid. Their fear was all that kept them in the bottle. Our fears can become the lids on our lives, too.

Consider the obstacles you've run up against recently. How did you handle them? Did you glance at the problem or gaze at the One with the power to solve the problem? God is bigger than any crisis you will confront. Even better, He is ready and willing to stand with you as you take it on.

Leaving Fear Behind

To move forward with the right perspective, it's essential to put aside your fears enough to clearly evaluate the risks you face. Renowned neurosurgeon Ben Carson knows all about evaluating high-stakes risk. When he was director of pediatric neurosurgery at Johns Hopkins Hospital, virtually every surgery he performed held profound risks, including the possibility of lifelong disability or death. With every surgery, he had to guide anxious parents through the difficult process of deciding whether or not to submit their children to operations that had the potential to improve their lives or end them. As part of his guidance, Dr. Carson encouraged parents to do what he called a Best/Worst Analysis:

- What is the *best* thing that can happen if I *do* this?
- What is the *worst* thing that can happen if I *do* this?
- What is the *best* thing that can happen if I *don't* do it?
- What is the *worst* thing that can happen if I *don't* do it?[3]

Dr. Carson's Best/Worst Analysis is useful because it forces us to identify what we're afraid of so we can weigh it against all that we have to gain. This kind of analysis is an essential component of keeping things in the right perspective. When you combine a prayerful analysis with a faith-based perspective, you'll have the freedom and confidence to decide whether or not a risk is worth taking. If you sense God is encouraging you to move ahead, then it's time to take action. Once you do, you'll most likely discover that your worst fears were unfounded. This has happened to me many times when I decided to trust God with a risky decision.

I faced one of the riskiest decisions I'd ever made when I was just twenty-six. Debbie and I had been married less than three years, and we'd just had our first child. I was a youth pastor at a growing church in Columbus and enjoyed leading the four hundred students who attended our programs each week. I had previously served for a summer as a youth pastor at a nearby church called Cascade Hills, and when they needed help to moderate a business meeting, they called me. It turned out that the pastor had just left, their membership was down to less than thirty people, and they needed help to make some decisions about their future.

A few weeks later, I showed up and led the meeting. Afterward, a handful of elderly folks approached me. One of them, a gentleman named William Graham, said, "Would you consider being our pastor?"

"Thank you, Mr. Graham," I said, "but no, I'm not really interested. I'm comfortable right now as a youth pastor. You need a pastor with experience."

A few days later, my pastor asked me to fill in for him and preach at our church for the next four weeks while he was out of town. I didn't have even two sermons developed, let alone four. I tried to turn down his request, but he and some of the deacons talked me into it. So I studied, put some messages together, and preached. To my surprise, it went so well and so many people welcomed Jesus into their hearts that it felt like a revival was under way!

That same month, I received a call from a church in Florida. A member of their congregation happened to have been visiting our church the week I gave the first of my four sermons and liked my preaching. They had just lost their pastor and had a question for me. Would I, the caller asked, be interested in becoming their pastor? Their offer included a generous salary and a down payment on a house. I thanked them for their offer and told them I'd consider it prayerfully and get back to them.

Later that same week, I got a call from a large church in Atlanta inviting me to consider a position there. That was followed a few days later by yet another invitation from a little church in the country. I had no idea what was going on. Just a few weeks earlier, I didn't even know four sermons to preach, and now I'd received offers from four churches to be their pastor.

Then I got another call from Cascade Hills. Would I reconsider their offer?

I told all the churches, including Cascade Hills, that I'd pray about their offer. I was definitely getting the message that God might be inviting me to make a move, but if so, where? The Florida church made the most sense financially. The Atlanta church offered important denominational and political connections. The little country church was located in a community that would be great for our growing family. The only church that didn't seem to have anything going for it was Cascade Hills, yet I sensed as I prayed that I should at least consider going there.

One morning, I read a Bible passage that made an impression on me:

> For you will go out with joy
> And be led forth with peace;
> The mountains and the hills will break forth into shouts of
> joy before you,
> And all the trees of the field will clap their hands. (Isaiah 55:12)

I didn't understand all of what that meant, but one of my Bible commentaries said the trees of the field represented the older, rooted members of the community. That pretty much described the remnant at Cascade Hills. I also noted that the name *Cascade Hills* seemed to connect with the verse's mention of mountains and hills. Admittedly, it wasn't a lot to go on, but I decided I would call one of the deacons at Cascade Hills, a man named Ross Bass, and ask to talk with him over lunch. He agreed.

"Mr. Bass," I said, "I don't know what to do. This church wants me. That church wants me. And Cascade Hills is asking me to come. I don't want to miss God's will, but I don't know how to make the right choice."

At that moment, the Lord spoke clearly to me. He said, *Watch his hands.*

What? I thought.

Watch his hands.

Mr. Bass leaned forward. "Brother Bill," he said, "our church is dying. We won't make it. We're going under and will close in a few months unless you come. If God would lead you to come to Cascade Hills"—he suddenly raised and clapped his hands once—"that would be wonderful."

That clap was like thunder in the room to me. I knew.

I left the meeting, sat in my car, and cried. "God," I said, "I'm afraid. I don't know what to do. If I go to Cascade Hills, I'll be leaving a secure job. I've got a family to take care of and I'm about to go home and tell Debbie that we're moving to a church that can hardly pay us. God, I don't know how or why, but I think I'm supposed to do it."

When my pastor returned after four weeks, I brought him up to speed on what was happening. "Pastor, I don't want to go," I said. "This is a good situation here. I'm getting great experience."

"Bill," he said, "you've been one of the best staff members I've ever had. I have total trust in you. As much as I don't want you to go, I would be getting in the way of God's plan if I tried to keep you. I can see it. The

deacons see it. You're the one who doesn't see it. I believe you need to go."
Then he quoted this verse: "The king's heart is like channels of water
in the hand of the LORD; He turns it wherever He wishes" (Prov. 21:1).
He followed the verse with a suggestion: "If you really want to know
if God's in this," he said, "tell them you'll preach one Sunday, but you
won't accept the position unless the congregational vote is 100 percent in
favor of you coming. If the vote is 100 percent, then you'll know without
a doubt it's God's will."

That made sense to me, and I put the whole thing in God's hands.
But when I told the Cascade Hills search committee about it, they sat
back in their chairs and shook their heads.

"Bill, you don't understand," one man said. "There's one family
here in the church that doesn't like you. They feel you have too much
zeal. They said if we bring you in, they'll vote against you. And we've
got another family with a relative about to graduate from seminary
who's looking for a church. They want him to be our pastor. So, Brother
Bill, you've already got two strikes against you."

"I'm sorry," I said. "That's what I've got to ask for." They still
wanted me to come preach, but they felt it would do little good.

Two weeks later, I showed up at Cascade Hills to preach on Easter
Sunday. Thirty-two people showed up. One of them, a tough karate
instructor named Jerry Cloud, walked up to the front of the church at
the end of my message and gave his heart to Jesus.

The congregational vote took place right after the service. I sat in an
office while the search committee tallied votes on my fate. Soon there
was a knock on the door and in walked a group of elderly men, all smil-
ing and looking as giddy as kids.

"One hundred percent!" one announced. "You got it!"

"Really?" I said. I couldn't believe what I was hearing. "What happened to the two families that were going to vote against me?"

I didn't learn the full answer to that question until a week later. One
family woke up Easter morning feeling too sick to come to church. But

they weren't worried—they knew the other family would still record a no vote. The other family, meanwhile, was walking to their car when friends from out of town unexpectedly pulled up. They decided to stay home with their company because they were sure the other family would vote down my candidacy. God arranged it so that neither family showed up in church that morning!

That move to Cascade Hills was definitely risky, and it didn't look very smart from the outside. I was already in a nice situation, and I had better reasons, at least on paper, to go elsewhere. Plus, I was afraid to go. But the more I thought about the best and the worst that could happen, I realized that I was more afraid *not* to go. I took the risk because I felt strongly that God was leading me there—but it was definitely a leap of faith. Just recently, when we celebrated Easter with more than ten thousand people at all our services, I realized again how taking that one risk launched me on an incredible journey. I have no regrets.

Your destiny awaits you if you are willing to break free of fear and take a God-honoring risk. If God is leading you, there's no safer place you could ever be, so take this promise from Scripture to heart: "Be strong and courageous! Do not tremble or be dismayed, for the LORD your God is with you wherever you go" (Josh. 1:9).

| **Insights for Inspiration** |

- A willingness to risk is essential to growth and success.
- Every good thing God offers begins with our willingness to risk.

Verse to Review

*"Do not fear, for I am with you; do not anxiously
look about you, for I am your God. I will strengthen
you, surely I will help you, surely I will uphold you
with My righteous right hand"* (Isa. 41:10).

Getting Personal

- How would you describe your risk style overall? In what ways has it influenced your decision making recently?

- How have the risks you've taken, or not taken, impacted your faith?

- Briefly recall an experience you consider a failure. What did you learn from that experience? How did it shape you or influence your perspective on risk?

- What risks do you sense God might be inviting you to take in this season of your life? How does Dr. Carson's Best/Worst Analysis influence your view of these risks?

The End of Excuses

The only man who is really free is the
one who can turn down an invitation to
dinner without giving an excuse.

Jules Renard

So far, we've talked about faith, prayer, vision, and the need to over-come fear in order to reach your full potential. The truth is, however, that even if you're progressing in each of these areas, there's one behavior that can still stop you in your tracks if you let it. It's a culprit that often takes the form of two little words: *if* and *but*. I'll bet you've used them a time or two. I know I have. Do statements like these sound familiar?

- *If* I had enough money, I could start the business I've always dreamed about.
- *If* I'd only been born with a more outgoing personality, I'd have more friends.
- I'd be a better parent, *but* I grew up in a dysfunctional family.
- I wanted to go to college, *but* no one gave me a chance.

There's only one word for these statements: *excuses*. They're the rationalizations we come up with to avoid taking legitimate responsibility for getting what we want out of life. Left unchecked, these excuses have the power to set the course for our future. I've seen people with incredible potential never realize their dreams because of excuses. I don't know who said it, but I know it is true: "Excuses are the enemies of excellence, the marks of mediocrity, and the forerunners of failure."

What's Your Story?

When we go through tough experiences in life—especially early in life—these formative experiences become our story. They create the framework for how we understand who we are and why we do what we do. When we use these hardships rightly, we can grow through them and use our story to help and inspire others. When we use them wrongly, we turn them into an excuse not to grow and use our story as a tool to manipulate others. If only we hadn't had such a bad childhood—a mean teacher, a slave-driving boss, a coldhearted spouse—then we would be so much farther along in life. I love the question leadership expert Tony Robbins often asks: "What is the story you keep telling yourself that gets in the way of your destiny?" Are such stories true? Maybe, but we can't live in an old story if we want to grow into a new one. If your story is an excuse for why you can't make it, you'll never fully live into your destiny.

I'm a big fan of mixed martial arts, and one of my favorite athletes is Frank Shamrock, former Ultimate Fighting Championship middleweight world champion. Frank is a great example of someone who refused to live locked down by excuses and his past. In his time, Frank Shamrock was "the man" in his sport. Because Frank has an enthusiastic and positive attitude, you'd never guess that his childhood was horrific. Among other things, his stepfather sometimes locked him in a closet all day while Frank's siblings ordered pizza and watched television or played in the yard. While in the closet, Frank peeked out of the crack at the bottom of the door and listened to the others laughing, talking, and acting as if he didn't exist.

It was in that closet, though, that Frank began to dream of a better life. He channeled his hurt by deciding he would one day become a world champion fighter. When he had the opportunity, he broke out of his old story and refused to use the difficult childhood he'd experienced as an excuse. He kept the dream born in a closet in front of him and worked hard until he reached it. Retiring from the ring in 2010, he's known today as Frank "The Legend" Shamrock.[1]

So what's your story? A marriage that fell apart? A promising job that turned into a layoff when the economy soured? An accident or illness that left you with debilitating injuries? A father who ran off when you were five? I don't mean to imply that these aren't devastating incidents—each is a blow that would knock anyone down. But when something like this happens to you, it's still only part of your story. You can allow it to keep you down, or you can use it as motivation to get back up. The way your story ends is up to you.

Exposing Excuses

Although they come in different shapes and sizes, all excuses have one thing in common: they enable us to avoid facing the truth. An excuse may not be an outright lie, but if we're honest, we have to admit that it's not the full truth either. A half-truth equals a whole lie. So in reality, we accuse ourselves when we excuse ourselves.

"Christian" excuses are among my favorites:

"I'm rude because I'm bold."
"I'm cheap because I'm a good steward."
"I'm critical because I'm a watchdog for error."
"I'm judgmental because I have discernment."

"I can't talk to people about Jesus or my faith because I'm not outgoing."

I actually had a man in our church parking lot tell me he couldn't share his faith because he was afraid to talk to strangers. Then he stepped into his truck, clicked on his CB radio, and said, "Breaker 1–9, anybody out there?" It seemed to me like he could talk to strangers just fine!

Do you see how all these excuses enable the speakers to avoid facing up to some hard truths about themselves? If they owned up to the truth, they might have to risk changing, and that's the one thing chronic excusers are desperate to avoid doing.

Over the years, I've discovered that people avoid facing up to the truth with excuses that typically fall into one of four categories: denial, detour, defense, or digging in.

1. *Denial.* This excuse is an outright lie. Although it may have elements of truth, you know it's denial because it usually sounds ridiculous. When Moses confronted Aaron about his part in making a golden calf for the Israelites to worship, Aaron said: "Do not let the anger of my lord burn. . . . They gave it [the gold] to me, and I threw it into the fire, and out came this calf" (Ex. 32:22–24). *Are you kidding me?* Can you believe Aaron actually said such a thing? It sounds ridiculous, right? But human beings still behave like this when they're desperate to avoid the truth.

2. *Detour.* This kind of excuse uses an indirect answer to avoid the truth. God, knowing Cain had murdered his brother, asked Cain where Abel was. Instead of giving a straightforward answer, Cain said, "Am I my brother's keeper?" (Gen. 4:9). He didn't lie, but he didn't tell the truth either.

3. *Defense.* This excuse is used to justify one's actions. Have you ever heard the saying, "Never ruin an apology with an excuse"? It's an attempt to acknowledge that I'm wrong while simultaneously avoiding the responsibility for what I've done: "I'm sorry, *but* . . ." This may be

the most dangerous and self-deceptive form of excuse. It's the tears without the desire to change. It looks like true repentance, but it's really just throwing empty words around in an effort to remove the pressure of guilt. When the prophet Samuel accused Saul of disobeying God by not destroying all of the Amalekites' animals in battle, Saul justified his actions with this excuse: "The people spared the best of the sheep and oxen, to sacrifice to the LORD your God; *but* the rest we have utterly destroyed" (1 Sam. 15:15, emphasis added). In other words, *Lord, I may not have done what You asked, but I disobeyed with good motives—I wanted to honor You.* What?!

4. *Digging In.* This form of excuse is more subtle. Many of us are plagued in this life by either guilt or bitterness—guilt over what we've done wrong or bitterness over how someone has wronged us. Some of us, unconsciously, use our obsession with guilt or bitterness as an excuse for avoiding what God wants for us and staying where we are.

Elaine was such a person. When she was sixteen, Elaine got pregnant. Her parents were disappointed and ashamed. Elaine wasn't ready to be a mother. She was so overwhelmed and distraught that an abortion seemed the only solution. She didn't tell her parents about it until after it was done.

After high school, Elaine fell in love with a young man named Steve. They married and moved to the West Coast to start their lives together, but the marriage was difficult right from the start. When they tried without success to have children, it only intensified the guilt Elaine carried about the abortion and increased the strain on her marriage. Night after night, she felt tormented by her conscience. *What was I thinking? I killed my child. I threw away the only chance I'll ever have for a son or daughter. How could I have been so blind? What will I tell my precious boy or girl when we meet in heaven? How can I ever justify what I've done?* Elaine knew God offered forgiveness for her actions and the chance to move on, but she chose instead to nurse her guilt.

Elaine never shared her secret or her struggles with Steve. That built a wall between them, and in the end, both of them were deeply hurt by it. One day, Steve confronted Elaine. Their relationship had no life to it, he said. They'd grown apart. After more than thirty years of trying to make it work, the marriage was over. He'd found someone else and was moving out.[2]

I'm not condoning what Steve did, and I do feel sympathy for Elaine's situation. But I also have no doubt that Elaine's secrecy and constant brooding over her abortion for more than three decades created a wedge between her and her husband. Her refusal to do the hard work of coming to terms with her guilt became an obstacle that contributed to the failure of her marriage. If Elaine had faced the issue, gotten help through counseling, and most importantly accepted God's forgiveness, the outcome might have been different. She chose to remain a victim of her past rather than face the truth that she did not trust God with her future.

Then there's the story of a man named Bob. His brother, Eldon, had secretly persuaded their elderly mother to sign over all her possessions to him. When she died, Eldon sold everything—their mother's house, furniture, cars, and rental properties—and disappeared with the money.

Not surprisingly, Bob was both devastated and furious. "I just wish I knew where he was," he said. "I'd like to get my hands on him just once. He's ruined my life. I just want a few minutes to ruin his, too." Bob, who'd been a cheerful guy with a reputation for practical jokes all his life, began telling fewer jokes and instead breaking out in more angry outbursts. In conversations, he constantly rehashed what his mother and brother had done, deepening his sense of betrayal and stoking his anger. Bitterness was eating away at his soul.[3]

When someone hurts us, it's natural to be angry. It's also natural to want to strike back. Like Bob, we might lick our wounds by constantly reliving the experience. We use our hurt as an excuse to stay angry. The truth, however, is that God doesn't want us to be controlled by anger; He wants us to give our anger to Him. If you nurse your hurt and rehearse the terrible thing that caused it, bitterness will take root, and that's a state you never want to live in. People who are bound by bitterness are miserable. They can't enjoy life. And the longer someone is bitter, the more destructive it is to their health, their relationships, and their future.

As a kid, I used to watch *Amos 'n' Andy* comedy on TV (yes, I'm that old!). I still remember an episode in which the two main characters were trying to solve a problem. "Amos," Andy said, "I'm tired of Kingfish always slapping me on my back. But I've got a solution for it."

"What's that?" Amos said.

"Look up under my coat. I've got three sticks of dynamite taped to my back. When he slaps me on the back this time, he's going to blow his hand off."

The joke, of course, is that the dynamite will hurt Andy as much as, if not more than, Kingfish. That's the problem with bitterness. It's like an acid that eats away the container that carries it. When we give in to bitterness, it hurts us more than the person we're angry with.

Whatever our excuses, the bottom line is that we often use them to justify our thoughts, words, and actions—sometimes without even realizing it. Think back on the last month. Have you employed any excuses lately? What truth about yourself might you be avoiding? This might be a good time to talk to God about it. He's not waiting to condemn you. He just wants you to confess it so He can forgive you and so you can get back on track and moving toward your destiny.

Fighting Back with Truth

Until God opened my eyes after my conversion, excuses were practically my lifestyle. "Everybody does it" was the standard excuse I used to justify anything I wanted to do. But that mindset just kept me trapped in self-deception. It never let me break out and find my purpose.

Everything changed the night I held on to that light pole and cried out to God. In the days and weeks that followed, He allowed me to see my existence from a whole new and true perspective. For the first time, I saw how I was wasting my life, how aimless and shortsighted I was. I saw that I'd been chasing after anything and everything to fill my emptiness, and that it seemed right at the time because everybody else did it, too. Now my eyes were open. I saw that pursuing God first provided the deepest level of fulfillment.

That was a game-changer for me. I became aware that my spiritual life, my relationships, and all that my life entailed had a lot to do with my own decisions. Because I felt accepted by God, I could finally break out of the mold I'd been in and grow in all areas of my life, whether everybody else was doing it or not. My fears and excuses had been holding me back, but no more. I finally saw the truth.

Truth is the most powerful weapon we have against an avalanche of excuses. It takes courage to be honest with yourself about your explanations and alibis, but it is the only way to be free of them. And we need this kind of truth whether the excuses are big cover-ups or small fibs. A mom of toddler twins named Kimberlee Conway Ireton had to come to terms with the routine excuses she made in everyday life. She once put off listening to a pair of phone messages for a day only to discover they were from the director of her children's homeschool co-op about an urgent matter. Kimberlee immediately called back and apologized for not responding sooner. But before she could stop herself, she lied to excuse the delay by saying that the twins had hidden her phone.

Some people would rationalize that excuse as a "white lie," a harmless fib that hurt no one. But not Kimberlee. For years, she'd been making up these kinds of excuses to avoid losing the approval of others. Regardless of whether they hurt anyone else, Kimberlee knew she was hurting herself with the lies. With every falsehood, she found it easier to tell another. Over time, she felt like she was turning into someone she didn't want to be.

Not long before the call from the co-op director, however, she'd developed a new strategy to fight her excessive excuses. It was based on the words of author and pastor Dallas Willard: "In the hurly-burly of life I may not be able to speak the truth always. But, as a discipline, I can perhaps make myself return to those to whom I have lied and tell them I misled or deceived them. This, in turn, will marvelously enhance my ability to speak the truth on other occasions."[4]

At the next co-op meeting, Kimberlee pulled the director aside and admitted to her fib. The director gave her a smile and a hug. Because Kimberlee confessed and switched from an excuse to the truth, the incident actually *increased* the director's trust in Kimberlee.[5]

You might want to try Kimberlee's approach. When you're tempted to create an excuse, remember the words of Dallas Willard. And if you've already used an excuse, go to the person you've misled and tell the real story. Making excuses traps you in a vicious cycle of seeking acceptance rather than truth. On the other hand, an honest admission allows others to view your transparency as a sign of strength. Ultimately, you have more freedom because there isn't the burden of creating and sustaining a false image for everyone around you.

There is something about transparency that attracts people. In the early days of my ministry, most of the pastors I met seemed to be perfect. In fact, they seemed so far removed from the kinds of struggles and failures I was dealing with that I felt guilty just being in their presence. But I will never forget a meeting I had with one nationally known pastor who showed me the power of transparency. One day over lunch he said, "Bill, I want to be honest with you. I've really been struggling with a problem." I thought he was going to tell me about a difficult leadership issue or a problematic staff member. I was shocked when he said, "I've really been struggling with the temptation of lust."

"What?" I said. "You deal with those things? Let me tell you, I have some struggles of my own." This man wasn't a weak leader. He was human, just like me—and he wasn't afraid to admit it. I watched him walk wisely through that season in his life and learned from his example. I believe that's why people are attracted to his leadership. They see his humanity in his honesty, and they respect him for it. I learned from him that strength is not covering up your imperfections but being humble enough to acknowledge them—to yourself and others.

Years ago, I was stopped by a policeman for speeding. I decided not to use any excuses. When the officer asked, "Mr. Purvis, why were you in such a hurry?" I answered in all honesty, "Because I didn't know you were around."

He laughed and said, "Well, I've heard story after story and lie after lie all day, but you are the first person who just came out and told me the truth." Now, I should not have been speeding—I was guilty of that—but because the officer respected my honesty, he didn't write me a ticket. That was nice.

I'll be the first to admit, however, that being honest is rarely the easiest choice. There are consequences to telling the truth, which is precisely why we rely on excuses. The truth hurts—especially when it's about our own failures and shortcomings. However, the truth also frees. Facing the truth about yourself and owning up to your imperfections will take the weight of the world off of your shoulders. Life only gets harder when we try to balance lie on top of lie and come up with new excuses for new circumstances. That will drain all the joy from your life. Peace comes only from the truth, and while getting there may not be easy, the peace that comes from knowing you have nothing to hide is always worth it. Don't give in to a pattern of easy excuses. Fight back with the truth.

A Winning Attitude

The final area we must master to end all excuses is our attitude. The truth is that it's not how hard our childhood was or what side of the tracks we were raised on or what happened to us that limits us. It's our attitude that limits or liberates us.

126

I first noticed this as a teenager. I took a job after school at a service station. I changed oil, tires, and car parts. The owner's name was Buck. He was Mr. Positive Attitude. He would look at a pouring-rain storm and talk about how great the day was going to be. I never saw him down. What made him even more impressive was how he treated his wife. Louise had had a stroke early in their marriage. Every weekend Buck took her out on a date. He'd bathe her, dress her, put her in a wheelchair, take her to dinner, feed her, and walk her through the side streets of our little town while pointing out things in the store windows. I used to wonder how someone could work so hard, give so much all the time, and never complain. Buck had a hard life, but I never heard him make an excuse for giving less than his best to the people around him.

If I ever messed up at work or made a mistake, which was common, Buck would say, "That's all right, Bill; it happens to the best of us." He never made an issue about it. I admired the way he used a great attitude to overcome circumstances. If he asked how someone was doing and they answered, "I'm doing pretty good under the circumstances," Buck would fire back, "Well, what are you doing under there?" He just refused to let negative thoughts or people control his thinking and life. I've lived long enough now to know that our past is no excuse for a bad attitude. A good attitude is a choice, and it's the best way to get past your past.

You cannot go forward by looking backward. I know two brothers who grew up with an alcoholic, abusive father. One son became an alcoholic early in life, couldn't keep a job, and abused his own children. The other son became a responsible family man, loved his wife and children, and never touched a drink. When they explained their present circumstances to the same counselor on separate occasions, both brothers had the same answer for their life: "If you had been raised by my father, you couldn't have turned out any other way." One used his past as his excuse for failure. The other used the same past as his motivation to be different.

We often think that successful people have abilities or opportunities that we didn't. The reality is just the opposite. They've had just as many obstacles to overcome as we have. Consider the excuses that could have stopped these successes:

- Heather Whitestone, named Miss America in 1994, is deaf.
- Wayne Gretzky, the hockey superstar, was fifty pounds lighter than the average player when he first tried out for the pros.
- Marathoner Joan Benoit, the 1984 Olympic gold medalist, underwent knee surgery seventeen days before that year's Olympic Trials.
- Marc Zupan, gold medalist in wheelchair rugby at the 2008 Beijing Paralympic Games, is a quadriplegic.
- Jean-Dominique Bauby, author of the 1997 release *The Diving Bell and the Butterfly*, dictated his book one eye-blink and one letter at a time after suffering a massive stroke.
- Pakistan's Malala Yousafzai, an activist for educating girls and winner of the 2014 Nobel Peace Prize at age seventeen, survived an assassination attempt by the Taliban in 2012.

It's been said that whiners see a problem in every opportunity while winners see an opportunity in every problem. This reminds me of two shoe salesmen who were sent to another country to market their shoes. One called back and said, "Get me on the next flight home. No one here wears shoes." The other salesman called his company and said, "Send me everything you have in stock. No one here wears shoes—this market's wide open!" Both salesmen were in the same circumstances. One saw a problem and came up with an excuse for failure. The other saw an opportunity and made plans to succeed.

Several years ago, I saw a different kind of opportunity. Some single mothers told me how hard it was to raise their sons without a male influence. They were concerned that their sons lacked athletic skills and had low self-images because they were behind in comparison to their peers. I wanted to be a part of their solution, so I volunteered to coach a baseball team. I asked a great big guy named Ed to help me.

On tryout day, Ed couldn't go, so I went alone. I saw that kids with few skills were not being picked, so I decided then and there to go after the kids no one else wanted. When I finally had a team, I called them together. They looked like kids from a refugee camp—skinny, scared, and awkward. The next day at the ball field, Ed walked up and said, "Where did you get those boys? We have to take them to one of those all-you-can-eat places. These kids should be on IVs or something."

It would have been easy for those boys, as well as for Ed and me, to make excuses about how poor our season was going to be. But Ed and I had a game plan. We decided to treat our boys like kings. We applauded everything they did. We celebrated everything they did, from arriving early to the way they kept their shirttails tucked in to who had the best attitude. We gave them positive nicknames. It became the happiest group of boys I'd ever seen. Anytime one of them did something well, we told the others to celebrate and congratulate him. It worked, too. Things started to jell. They started feeling good about themselves, and it showed on the field. Instead of creating excuses for not trying, they played their hearts out and began to beat teams no one believed they could beat.

The breakthrough came when a boy named Josh, who'd always had raw talent buried underneath, hit a ball over the fence and clinched the win for us in a playoff game. He came around third base with the biggest smile and hugged me like a bear. This was his first home run. After the game, Josh handed me the ball as a gift, and I asked him to sign it for me. The season ended with us at the top, but more importantly, I saw firsthand how a winning attitude puts an end to excuses.

To break out of the mold and pursue a new future, you have to realize that your days are temporary and that you must make changes now. We may get out of a problem with an excuse, but we can't stay out of problems without a change. The change in your attitude is crucial. People who become the best are no better than the rest. They beat the rest simply because they refuse to settle for anything less than the best.

Exchanging Our Excuses for God's Promises

One of the greatest leaders in the Bible started out with the wrong attitude. Moses had a confidence problem. When God came to him and asked him to lead the Israelites out of Egypt, Moses immediately made excuses: "I'm not good enough. The people won't believe me. I'm not a good speaker. They won't listen to me." Even after God gave him the ability to do miraculous signs, he kept making excuses. God's response to Moses' excuses was "I AM."

I am what? Moses probably thought. It's an incomplete sentence. God left it that way on purpose. Moses had to fill in the blank: "I am . . . whatever you need. I am your peace if you need it. I am your strength if you need it. I am your provider if you need it."

The same promise is still available to us today. For every step of faith I have ever taken there have been a dozen good excuses for not doing so. You have to be the one to eliminate your excuses. The amazing thing is that once Moses quit making excuses, God started eliminating his problems. When Moses made the decision to go back to Pharaoh, God had Moses' brother, Aaron, meet him on the way to help him speak. Aaron also made the Hebrew people believers (Ex. 4:27–31).

One of the best ways to quit making excuses is to take action. "I AM" didn't mean anything to Moses until he stood in front of Pharaoh and the Hebrew people. This is when he needed God to come through for him—and He did. God still makes His promises available to us, but they're useless until we act on them.

I once heard about a very old woman who died alone in her house. When city officials found her, they contacted her only son and told him that his mother died of starvation. "That's impossible!" the son said. "I've been sending her money every week for months." But when he arrived at her home to collect her belongings, he noticed that all of the money orders he'd been sending were pinned up on the walls. His mother never realized what they were. She didn't understand how to use them. She thought they were just nice cards from her son.

We also are headed for trouble when we fail to use God's promises. God did not give us His promises to put on our desks, our shirts, our car bumper, or the wall. He gave them to us to act on, to cash in, to prove. In fact, He doesn't call us to do anything without sending His provision to do it. Where He guides, He provides.

It's still our choice whether we break out and change or not. We can stay in the same place blaming everyone else for the condition we're in, or we can take responsibility for our actions and move ahead.

God's gift to us is our life. Our gift to Him is what we do with it. I live by the motto that if you do what you can with what you have, where you are, God will not leave you where you are, and He will increase what you have. I have seen this work for people who started with nothing and who started late in life. For anything you think you want to do in life, if it's not important to you, you will find an excuse not to do it. But if it's important to you, you will find a way to make it happen!

Insights for Inspiration

- Facing the truth is a powerful weapon against excuses.

- Paying the price to succeed early on ensures rewards you want later on.

- God's name "I AM" reminds us that He's sufficient for whatever we need.

Verse to Review

"The LORD is near to all who call upon Him, to all who call upon Him in truth" (Psalm 145:18).

Getting Personal

- Briefly recall a recent excuse you made. Was it for something you'd done or for something you wanted to avoid doing?

- Which of the four categories of excuses—denial, detour, defense, digging in—do your excuses tend to fall into? Why?

- How do you think your life might be different if you were able to cut out the excuses and humbly tell the truth instead?

- Generally speaking, are you more likely to pay now and play later, or to play now and pay later?

═══ 8 ═══

Strength from Within

Character is a diamond that
scratches every other stone.

Cyrus A. Bartol

When the pressure is on, what's inside always comes out. In a crisis or under stress, we don't have the luxury of keeping up appearances. It's at such times that our actions reveal who we really are—for good or for ill. Allow me to share two stories that demonstrate what this looks like in everyday life.

Author and pastor Tim Kimmel was on a hunting trip with his friend Tom, a family man and leader in Tim's church. Around the campfire that first night, Tom opened up about a heartbreaking situation—his teenage daughter had become pregnant.

Tim asked if they had decided to keep the baby or put it up for adoption.

"We considered the alternatives, Tim," Tom said. "Weighed all the options. We finally made an appointment with the abortion clinic. I took her down there myself."

Tim couldn't believe what he was hearing. For years, Tom had been a vocal opponent of abortion. He'd even volunteered at a crisis pregnancy center.

"I know what I *believe*, Tim," Tom said, "but that's different than what I had to *do*. I had to make a decision that had the least amount of consequences for the people involved."

Tim sensed his friend had rehearsed those lines. The look in Tom's eyes and emptiness in his voice showed that he knew how unconvincing his words sounded.[1] When the pressure was on, the true nature of his beliefs came out.

Like Tom, Todd Pierce was a man of faith. For six years, he was among the world's best professional bareback horsemen and competed in rodeos across the United States. When continuing injuries forced him to retire from competition, Todd became a pastor for the Professional Bull Riders organization.

Most of Todd's ministry involved talking with bull riders, encouraging them as husbands and fathers, and urging them to lead godly lives. But during one rodeo in Southern California, the stakes got much higher. Todd had just helped a veteran rider named B. J. Kramps mount a bull in the bucking chute. Once Kramps entered the arena, the bull bucked Kramps off his right side. The cowboy tried to get up and scramble away, but the rope tied around the bull's belly had rolled over his hand and Kramps was caught.

The bull dragged and kicked Kramps across the arena and back to the bucking chute. Three men in charge of protecting riders frantically gave chase but couldn't catch up with the bull.

Oh my gosh, Todd thought, *B.J.'s gettin' killed*. He knew it was time to act.

When the fifteen-hundred-pound bull thundered near the bucking chute, Todd leapt from the six-foot fence over the bull's back and at the same time tried to grab the rope that trapped Kramps. He missed and fell to the ground.

The bull stopped just twenty feet away, turned, and charged.

Todd hustled to his feet. At the last instant, he jumped onto the bull's head, desperately twisting to avoid two deadly horns while also grabbing again for the rope.

This time he got it. Todd and one of the other men in the arena were able to turn the rope and free Kramps. Todd covered Kramps with his body while the others distracted and then corralled the bull. Amazingly, Kramps suffered no major injuries.[2]

In a moment of crisis, Todd's heart for his fellow cowboys was on display for all to see. When the pressure was on, who he was inside came out.

So what is it that bubbles to the surface when we're strained to the breaking point? *Character.* Character is the ability to live out the principles and values we believe in and aspire to. Tim Kimmel's friend Tom believed in the sanctity of life, but when he faced a crisis, his character wasn't strong enough to live out that value. Todd Pierce also believed in the sanctity of life. But unlike Tom, it was a value so deeply rooted within him that risking his life to save B. J. Kramps was the most natural thing in the world for him to do. His character was as strong as the values he believed in.

Strong character is a nonnegotiable requirement for achieving our goals and dreams. It is the battering ram that allows us to break through obstacles and grow into a better life. Every challenge we face on the journey to a better life has the potential to either take us down or make us stronger. There's no middle ground. When we face problems and hard times, it's the strength of our character that enables us not only to face the storm but to turn it to our advantage.

If I've convinced you about the importance of character, you might be thinking, *Great! I'm all in. How do I get a strong character?* I'm so glad you asked. As with virtually every other area of growth, we strengthen our character by exercising it. Are you ready for a workout? The gym for character is everyday life, and the strength-training weights we lift are the daily challenges, temptations, and decisions we face—both small and large. The apostle Paul describes it this way: "We also exult in our tribulations, knowing that tribulation brings about perseverance; and perseverance, proven character; and proven character, hope" (Rom.

5:3–4). Did you catch that progression? The path to proven character begins with tribulations (hardships and suffering) and develops into perseverance (the ability and determination to stick it out) before it grows into character. In other words, if we want strong character, we can be glad we have some problems because persevering through them is the only way we're going to get it. It's a truth I had to learn the hard way in the early years of my marriage and my ministry.

When Debbie and I first got married, we were madly in love and spent every minute we could together. But as my ministry grew, I began to pour most of my time and energy into being the best pastor I could— which meant I spent less time and energy being the best husband I could. By the time we started having kids, I was devoting so much of my time to ministry that I tended to leave the responsibilities of parenting to Debbie and didn't pay much attention to her needs or the condition of our marriage.

I had packed my bags and was about to head out the door for a speaking engagement one afternoon when Debbie's face fell. "You're leaving again?" she said.

"Yeah," I said. "I'm speaking tonight at a pastors' conference. I'll be back in the morning." That was the end of the conversation—I had to get going.

At the conference, I sat at a table and mentally rehearsed a few of the things I planned to talk about while the pastor speaking just before me addressed the crowd. However, as the speaker continued, I forgot all about my speech. I felt as if he were speaking directly to me.

"If you don't take care of your home life," the man said, "you don't have anything to speak about. You don't have anything to say. Your credibility is your family. If you win the world for Christ but lose your family, everything you've done doesn't matter."

You know, I thought, *I'm not doing this right.* I realized that instead of growing into a loving, intimate relationship, my marriage was turning into a partnership of convenience—I'd earn the money if she'd manage the house and the kids. *I'm gonna encourage a room full of strangers tonight while my wife and I are strangers. I'm giving more to these pastors than I am to her.*

I turned to the pastor who had organized the event and said, "Look, you're going to have to get somebody to take my place. I can't speak."

The pastor's eyes widened. "No, Bill," he said. "You're up next."

"I can't," I said. "What that guy just said really hit me. I'm not going to be a hypocrite and go up there. I've got to leave."

I know the pastor wasn't happy about it, but that's just what I did. I got up and headed straight home. When I walked in the door, Debbie was still up.

"I thought you were gone tonight," she said, a surprised look on her face.

I didn't waste time with explanations. I walked over to my wife and got on my knees.

"Debbie, I want you to forgive me," I said. "I wanted you, pursued you, and married you. But I know I haven't made our marriage a priority. I let work get in the way. I've been so busy that I've neglected our marriage. Will you forgive me?"

That night marked a turning point in our marriage. I began focusing more on Debbie and investing myself more intentionally in our marriage. I changed the way I spent my time so I could restore a healthy balance between the demands of home and work. Debbie and I also developed mentoring friendships with couples who had strong marriages, which helped us to learn how to better communicate.

What I didn't realize prior to the pastors' conference was that the pressure of a stagnant marriage had been building up inside me. When I heard that speaker's words about family and credibility, the pressure was too much, and I had to do something about it—what was inside had to come out. My actions would either move my marriage forward or inch it closer to inevitable disaster. I easily could have pushed aside what my heart was telling me by allowing pride and the need to keep up appearances to send me to the podium.

Fortunately for me, God had been working on my character—helping me to grow through other problems and challenges. I had just enough sense to drop what I was doing, get home, and start taking steps that would change the course of my family's life forever. After thirty-five years of marriage, three kids, and six grandchildren, I am so grateful for that breakthrough.

How about you? What comes out when you're under pressure? Is your character moving you forward, helping you get where you want to go—and where God wants you to go? Or is it holding you back, preventing you from living out your values and realizing your dreams?

Let's talk more about good character—what it is and how you can get it.

The Little Things

In 1986, schoolteacher Christa McAuliffe and six other crew members boarded the space shuttle *Challenger* for what was to be a historic mission. When the shuttle exploded seventy-three seconds into its flight, leading to the deaths of all seven crew members, the watching world was shocked and horrified. But the greater shock came later when the failure of an inexpensive rubber O-ring was identified as the cause of the explosion. Due to the unusually cold weather that morning, the small gasket became brittle and cracked, leaking fuel and leading to the tragedy. One tiny crack triggered a disaster the world will never forget.

It's a tragic story, but it illustrates a foundational principle: little things have great power. When it comes to character, how we respond to little challenges and problems will ultimately determine whether we reach our dreams or self-destruct in the process.

So what kind of "little things" are we talking about? They're the kind of things about which you might think, *It's not harming anyone. No one will ever even know.* For example, maybe you see no problem with occasionally using the postage meter at work to pay for personal mail. Perhaps you justify making calls and sending emails to friends during work hours, or you sometimes help yourself to office supplies. But all those little things, however insignificant they seem, do add up. From pilfering to embezzlement, the American economy loses billions annually from workplace theft and diminished productivity. When we behave this way, it's not just our employers who pay a cost. Little cheats and transgressions lower your guard, dull your conscience, and set the stage for a big crash in your integrity. When you're tempted to compromise on something no one will ever know about, consider the wise advice of Thomas Jefferson: "Ask yourself how you would act were all the world looking at you, and act accordingly."[3]

I once visited a patient at the local medical center where the parking fee was fifty cents. As you exit the parking lot, you put your quarters in a parking meter and an electric gate rises to let you drive through. On this particular occasion, I didn't even have a nickel. A friend in the parking lot let me drive through behind him before his gate came down. I promised him I would come back and pay the fifty cents. Of course, he thought I was crazy to drive back across town for fifty cents no one would ever know about. And I guess it probably did look strange when I returned, inserted my fifty cents in the meter, and stood there watching the electric gate go up and down. But I had to do it. Stealing is stealing, even if it's only fifty cents. And I truly believe that every seed I plant today is a harvest I will reap tomorrow. It didn't matter that no one but me would ever know; I was making a choice to invest in and strengthen my character. And my character is worth infinitely more to me than fifty cents.

When we are willing to compromise on everyday choices, we are choosing to live by selective integrity. The foundational principle of selective integrity is that only "big" things are wrong; the little things don't really count. For example, an extramarital affair is wrong, but the occasional flirtation with a married person is okay. Fraud is wrong, but slightly under-reporting income on your taxes is okay. Gossip is wrong, but sharing inappropriate information about someone in the form of a "prayer request" is okay. Success at any cost is wrong, but neglecting family to catch up with work on the weekends is okay. You see the problem with this line of thinking, right? Every one of those little things weakens your character, which means you won't have the strength of character you need to deal with the big things when they come—and they will come.

I battled the issue of selective integrity once when I bought a car several years ago in Mobile, Alabama. The dealership called and wanted me to lie on a form—to say I paid the taxes in Alabama instead of Georgia, where I live. With some simple paperwork—a small thing—I could save myself $1,100. On top of that, the dealer made it clear that eighty-seven people had already done it. When I refused to go along with his request, he got angry. I guess he was afraid he'd be exposed. He begged me to comply, repeating over and over that eighty-seven other people had done it.

"Look," I finally said, "I don't care if eighty-seven other people have done it. I'm not doing it!" The whole time he was begging me to give in, I was thinking, *Why should I lose integrity and God's favor because everyone else did this?* In matters of conscience and character, the law of majority does not matter.

You'll never develop strong character if you compromise your integrity. Integrity is about being honest and having strong principles, but it is also defined as being whole and undivided. In other words, there is nothing "selective" about real integrity—it's all or nothing. Either you have it or you don't. When we have integrity, there is no difference between our beliefs and behavior, how we respond to little compromises and big compromises, or what we do when others are watching or not watching.

So how can you maintain your integrity and strengthen your character in the little things? When you're uncertain about a decision or a course of action, step back and carefully work through questions like these:

- Is there a clear right or wrong?
- Even if other people think it's right, does it meet God's standards for right?
- Would my choice set a good example?
- Is my choice driven by what's easiest or most convenient for me, or by my integrity?
- Will this choice move me closer to or farther from the kind of person I want to be?
- If this choice is a seed, what harvest might I reap from it in the days, weeks, or years to come?

Do you feel the weight—the strength-training weight—of these questions? When you use them to work through the routine choices of everyday life, you're exercising and strengthening your character. Over time, your character muscles will be strong enough that doing the right thing comes easily and naturally; you won't have to give it much thought even when the stakes are high.

That's what happened once to professional racquetball player Reuben Gonzalez. The stakes could not have been higher—match point in the final game of his first professional tournament. With a super "kill shot" into the front wall, Gonzalez defeated the reigning champion and won the tournament. The referee called the shot good. One of the linesmen affirmed that the shot was in. But Gonzalez, after a moment's hesitation, shook his opponent's hand and declared that his shot had first hit the floor before skipping into the wall. As a result, he lost the championship. When asked why he did it, Reuben said, "It was the only thing I could do and maintain my integrity."[4]

There's no doubt that choosing integrity may cost you something in the short term, but here's another way to look at it. Your integrity is priceless. Whatever it costs you to keep it is a bargain. That's why Reuben Gonzalez could make the choice that he did. A tournament win was too cheap a prize to exchange for his integrity. When you have the strength of character to do right in the little things, you develop the strength of character you need to do right in the big things later on.

Insights for Inspiration

- Pressure will eventually force us to reveal who we are on the inside.

- Strong character is the battering ram that allows us to break through obstacles and grow into a better life.

- How we respond to "little" character challenges today will have a big impact tomorrow.

- It takes time to build a strong, lasting foundation of character.

Verse to Review

"The LORD does not look at the things people look at. People look at the outward appearance, but the LORD looks at the heart" (1 Sam. 16:7 NIV).

Getting Personal

- Briefly recall a recent experience when you were under pressure or faced a crisis. What "came out" of you in that experience? What did it reveal about your character?

- On a scale of one to ten (one being low, ten being high), how would you assess the strength of your integrity when it comes to the "little things" in life?

- What do you find most motivating about the promise of a strong character? What is it you most hope to experience by strengthening your character?

Choose Your Mentors Well

Be imitators of me, just as I also am of Christ.
1 Corinthians 11:1

Back when I was in high school, a lot of my friends played in the Eufaula pool halls, so I went, too. I wasn't very good, but I wanted to be. The owner of one of those places, an old man nicknamed Slick, had once been a pool shark. He'd often say, "You don't have to make all the mistakes yourself. Watch the rest of the players and see what they do. The way you learn this game is you go to school on another man's shot."

That's what I did. I observed what happened when the best players shot—where the ball went, how they held their sticks, how far they leaned over the table. When it was my turn to shoot, I already had a mental picture of what worked and what I wanted to do. It made me a better player.

I never forgot Slick's sage advice: "Go to school on another man's shot." And I soon realized it was a principle I could apply in any area of life—finances, faith, marriage, or even building a church. Everyone had something to teach me, and the people who had overcome their mistakes and mastered their craft had the most to teach. The older I get, the more

I know how little I know. If you and I can learn from people who are ahead of us in the ways we want to grow, we won't have to repeat their mistakes. Instead, we can build on their success.

Many years ago when I was new to ministry, I was hungry to learn all I could from anyone who had something of value to teach me. I was a church staff member at the time, and after a well-known Christian leader had visited our church, I asked for the chance to drive him back to the airport in Atlanta. It was a ninety-minute trip, and I was determined to make the most of it, so I brought along a notebook with about sixty questions I wanted to ask him. The poor man had no idea what he was in for!

When I picked him up at the hotel, he sat in the backseat. I asked if he'd like to ride up front, but he declined. He went on to tell me that he felt ill and tired and didn't want to have conversation on the trip. I thought, *That's not going to happen.* I'd never held a great leader captive before, and I wasn't about to let him get away without giving me some of his wisdom and advice.

I waited until we were down the road a few minutes and then began asking him some of my questions. Out of courtesy, he answered them. And I actually took notes on what he said while driving! Then I asked a few more questions. He sighed and gave me more great answers. I waited a few minutes and asked again. After about forty-five minutes of this, he finally blew up.

"Are you a Philadelphia lawyer or something?" he screamed. I glanced in the rearview mirror and saw that his face was red. "I have never been interrogated and bombarded with so many questions in my life! Don't ask another question."

I looked down at my list. I still had three more questions, and we had forty-five minutes left. I let him cool down for about twenty minutes, and then I got the other three questions in. When we arrived at the airport, he practically jumped out of the backseat to escape my inquisition.

Several years later, I was teaching at a conference and that same gentleman approached me after my talk. He asked if I remembered our previous encounter and then apologized for his behavior. "At the time," he said, "I didn't realize how serious you were in asking me all those questions. I didn't believe you would use the advice, so I thought you were wasting my time. I prejudged you, and I'm sorry. Hearing you today, I realize you were searching and really were going to act on what you'd learned."

I apologized to him for being so relentless that day in the car. A few minutes later, both of us were laughing. As he walked away, I called to him. He turned. "Yes?" he said.

"Can I ask you a question?" I said in jest, a smile on my face. He threw up his hands in mock disgust and walked off.

As you pursue your dreams and the destiny God has for you, it's important to know that you don't have to do it all by yourself. In fact, seeking out teachers, mentors, and wise guides is essential. The Bible says, "Where there is no guidance the people fall, but in abundance of counselors there is victory" (Prov. 11:14). Your learning curve will increase exponentially when you go to school on the experience of others. You can and should do that by reading and studying, but there's no substitute for the kind of mentoring that happens when you can meet with someone face-to-face. That enables you to learn not just from what they know but also from who they are.

Making Your Mentor Choice

What should you look for in the people you want to learn from and approach for guidance? What makes someone a strong mentor? I've found the life and teachings of the apostle Paul to be a helpful model for knowing what a mentor should look like. Not only did Paul say, "Be imitators of me, just as I also am of Christ" (1 Cor. 11:1), but he also proved his character by living it out among those he taught. When it comes to identifying the important qualities of a mentor, I find this passage of Paul's especially helpful:

> You yourselves know, from the first day that I set foot in Asia, how I was with you the whole time, serving the Lord with all humility and with tears and with trials . . . how I did not shrink from declaring to you anything that was profitable, and teaching you publicly and from house to house. . . . I do not consider my life of any account as dear to myself, so that I may finish my course and the ministry which I received from the Lord Jesus. . . . I commend you to God and to the word of His grace, which is able to build you up and to give you the inheritance. . . ." (Acts 20:18–20, 24, 32)

What are some of the qualities of mentors that Paul describes here? There are four that stand out to me: humility, profitable teaching, a commitment to perseverance and finishing well, and reliance on God's power. Let's explore each in depth.

Humility

Humility is defined as having a modest view of one's own importance. When Paul says he served the Lord with "all humility," he uses a Greek phrase that conveys "lowliness of mind."[1] Because Paul considered everything he did to be "serving the Lord," he never adopted a superior attitude, even with those he taught and mentored. Instead, he demonstrated the heartfelt belief that God is the source of everything we have to offer, including wisdom and experience. That's humility.

I have the privilege of being the pastor to some outstanding and high-achieving people in our community. All of them have legitimate reasons to be proud of their accomplishments, and perhaps to expect some special treatment because of them. But the common trait I see in nearly all of them is a natural and easygoing humility. They don't act like they are entitled, and they never demand special treatment or recognition. Instead, their humble service demonstrates their belief that every blessing is a gift and that it's a privilege to serve God by serving others. Here are a few examples that inspire me.

- One humble servant is a medical doctor with Ivy League degrees and a state-of-the-art surgical center. He prays for each patient before performing surgery, asking for God's healing presence to be with them both as a way of acknowledging the One who is *really* in control of the outcome. Every week, he serves as a volunteer in our coffee shop at the church. His tone and demeanor reflect sincere humility.

- Another is a respected obstetrician and gynecologist. After working all week with moms and babies, he volunteers in our nursery on weekends. His servant heart reflects a humility that is highly attractive.

- Yet another of our church members readily donated $300,000 when he heard we needed to build a parking lot closer to our building. Even though he paid for the parking lot, he rides a shuttle each week from another lot a quarter mile away because he doesn't feel entitled to a better spot.

It's the humility of these people and many like them that allows me to see why God has entrusted them with so much.

When you're searching for a mentor, look for someone who has proven gifts, wisdom, or achievements, yet displays a humble spirit. Instead of using what God has blessed them with as a means of self-promotion or to secure special treatment, your mentor needs to be someone who readily uses what they have to serve others.

Jesus' disciples had some lessons to learn about humility in this regard. When Jesus found them arguing about position and greatness, He said:

You know that the rulers of the Gentiles lord it over them, and their great men exercise authority over them. It is not this way among you, but whoever wishes to become great among you shall be your servant, and whoever wishes to be first among you shall be your slave; just as the Son of Man did not come to be served, but to serve, and to give His life a ransom for many. (Matthew 20:25–28 NASB)

We need a humble mentor because we pick up more than knowledge from the people we spend time with. We also pick up their values, their attitude, and their spirit. I've spent years instilling this important lesson in my three boys. You don't take advice from or choose a mentor who isn't where you want to be. When looking for a couple to mentor you in your marriage, you look for two people who have weathered trials and come out stronger on the other side, not those who are teetering on the edge of divorce. You're not just trying to learn something new; you're hoping to become something new.

Profitable Teaching

When Paul said he "did not shrink from declaring to you anything that was profitable," he meant he'd made it a point to understand what the Ephesians most needed to hear and gave them that teaching. He made the effort to understand where his listeners were at and challenged them with valuable insights that would help them grow from that point.

True mentors take a genuine interest in you and love to celebrate your progress in life. I was fortunate to have such a person in my life from the beginning—my mother. Unlike my father, who felt threatened by my growth and achievements, Mom taught me anything and everything she thought might help me to grow. She always encouraged me, always wanted the best for me, and always believed in me.

I was also fortunate to have a friend named Ike Reighard, who introduced me to leadership expert and author John Maxwell. That day was a game-changer for me. John has no clue as to the impact he's had on me and my leadership.

Years ago, thanks to Ike, Debbie and I were scheduled to meet John Maxwell for the first time for dinner in Atlanta. I didn't sleep at all the night before. Only a few days prior, a group of pastors had shunned me at a luncheon. It hurt and confused me. As I lay in bed, I thought, *What if he treats me like those other pastors did?*

Fortunately, all my fears proved baseless. John treated Debbie and me as equals and friends. He asked about the growth of our little church and celebrated with us like it really mattered to him. By the end of our time together, I felt like he genuinely believed in me. He recognized it was exactly what I needed at that point in my life.

Debbie and I didn't sleep that night either, but this time it was excitement, not fear, that kept us awake. We couldn't stop talking about the possibilities and potential John said he saw in us. I'll never forget his words: "Bill, you have five thousand in you. Debbie, you have *ten* thousand in you." His reference to the numbers was about the lives he thought we could reach with the gospel. That encouraged me, because it meant that between the two of us we had the potential to help fifteen thousand people become new believers! Later, John invited me to speak at his Challenge 1000 conferences, and he always treated me with kindness whenever we met.

Years later, John's impact on my life also had an impact on my son Brent. One day when Brent was helping me move some books and boxes out of my home office, he came across an old set of one hundred cassette tapes, all featuring John talking about leadership. When Brent asked his mother what they were, she said, "He's the guy who changed a lot of things in your dad's life." Brent started listening to those tapes. He even had an old cassette player put in his car. In just thirty days, he'd listened to all one hundred tapes. Then he began buying all of John's books. In no time, Brent was looking at life through the eyes of a leader.

I have never seen anyone changed so radically so quickly. He went from a teenage boy who was interested mostly in big trucks and fast cars to a grown man ready to run an organization, laser-focused on his role in advancing the kingdom. A few weeks ago, as Brent was speaking to over ten thousand people at the city civic center, I thought again about how much he'd grown into a leader—all inspired by one man who knew just how to encourage a certain pastor and his wife.

That's what good mentors do—they recognize the meeting point between their wisdom and your needs and deliver teaching that is profitable in the moment. They find ways to show you how to grow.

Commitment to Perseverance and Finishing Well

Paul, the apostle formerly known as Saul, never did anything halfway. As Saul, he was among the best at persecuting Christians. Once he chose to follow Jesus, he was 100 percent committed to bringing Christ's message to the world. He said he did not consider his life of any account; as long as he still breathed, he would focus on finishing the job for Jesus.

Faithful people like Paul finish strong. They make good mentors and role models because the integrity of their actions and choices over time has proven their character.

This was especially important to Debbie and me when we sought out mentors to help us grow in our marriage. When Debbie and I were married, we had our love for each other but not much else—no life plan, no marriage plan, no plan of any kind. We didn't have role models, and we both came from homes without the best examples. Within a few years, we slowly grew apart. After I had my breakthrough experience at the pastors' conference and apologized to Debbie, we both knew we needed help. We needed mentors who had already persevered in their marriage and who were not only doing well but committed to finishing well.

We sought out another pastor and his wife, A. T. and Terri Stewart. The Stewarts had been married for fourteen years, and their love and respect for one another made it plain they had a healthy marriage. The way they communicated so openly with each other about sensitive topics without fear of stepping on landmines was refreshing. A. T. and Terri agreed to meet with us every Friday night for a few months. During that time, they opened our eyes to a world we'd never known. We learned how to communicate, how to listen, what each other's gifts and temperament were, why we made decisions the way we did, how to approach each other, and a host of other things. Each week was a crash course with an overload of information and assignments to work on for the next mentoring session. We not only listened to what A. T. and Terri said but also watched how they interacted and held on to every example they gave us. I can't tell you how many times A. T. rebuked me in his loud voice: "William, you're wrong!" Or how often he said to Debbie, "It's going to take a lot of patience to turn him around. Are you up for this?"

But all that mentoring paid off. Today, Debbie and I are more in love than ever. She's my best friend. We've built a thousand great memories, raised three awesome sons, and now have six incredible grandchildren. For the past few years, we've begun to "pay it forward" by offering an annual marriage retreat. Hundreds of couples attest each year to their own life-changing experience after attending the retreat and learning from our experience. I don't believe our marriage would have lasted even five years without A. T. and Terri's mentorship.

When you look for role models, seek out the ones who have perseverance and staying power. It doesn't take great skill to succeed in the short term. But when you meet people who have persevered through hardships and are continuing to grow and learn year after year, study them. Seek out their counsel, ask about their strategies and practices, and observe their way of life. You'll find it invaluable.

Reliance on God's Power

As great a teacher as Paul was, he never lost sight of the fact that it wasn't his words but God's grace that brought about lasting change and salvation: "I commend you to God and to the word of His grace, which is able to build you up and give you the inheritance" (Acts 20:32). Your best bet for obtaining the insights you desire is to pursue mentors who honor and rely on God's power for their teaching.

It takes trust for a mentor relationship to work. You might be able to overcome superficial differences with a mentor, but if you disagree on fundamentals such as your faith, it will be that much harder to trust the counsel you receive. This may be one of the reasons the Bible tells us, "Do not be bound together with unbelievers; for what partnership have righteousness and lawlessness, or what fellowship has light with darkness?" (2 Cor. 6:14). Jesus is our ultimate role model. The more our mentors reflect Him, the better off we'll be. Make sure you seek out a mentor who truly relies on God's power and grace and lives that out on a daily basis.

People may say that they depend on and follow God, but their actions may indicate something else. I once had breakfast with a well-known man I'd admired from a distance and was blown away by the demeaning way he treated his wife. He was cruel, insulting, disrespectful, and arrogant. Perhaps he thought belittling her would impress me. I watched her fight back tears, fake a laugh to hide her pain, and act as if she wasn't bothered, when it was obvious she was. The more I tried to compliment her, the worse he was. His need for attention at the expense of his wife immediately disqualified him as a mentor in my book. She'd made a vow to him, "Till death do we part," so I guess she was hanging in. But I didn't make that vow with him, so we parted company that day. You cannot really know people until you observe them up close.

Centuries ago, a woman in the Middle East received very different treatment. You probably know the New Testament story of the woman caught in the act of adultery. A group of Pharisees brought her to Jesus and asked what they should do, hoping to trap Jesus with His response. His response caught them off guard: "He who is without sin among you, let him be the first to throw a stone at her." The Pharisees dispersed one by one. When the woman acknowledged that no one was left to condemn her, Jesus said, "I do not condemn you, either. Go. From now on sin no more" (see John 8:1–11).

This is the kind of mentor you want—one who gets his wisdom from and displays the grace of God.

Integrity over Impressions

We've just reviewed four important qualities in a great mentor. There is another quality, however, that can make you forget about everything you've just learned when you're sizing up a potential mentor. I'm talking about a "star"—someone whose popularity or winning personality makes a great first impression, but who may or may not have the integrity to back it up.

It's easy to be starstruck, but don't throw away your common sense when you meet someone with power, influence, or expertise. No matter how gifted, popular, or smart someone is, until you really know something about that person's character—who they are when nobody's looking—you should exercise caution in seeking their guidance and input. Almost anyone can fake a good impression on special occasions, but it takes character to live a life of integrity day in and day out. So decide in advance to be starstruck by integrity rather than a flashy first impression.

Take a second look at people who make a flashy first impression. How do they treat other people? Do their actions line up with their words, or does it seem like they're always spinning the truth to make themselves look better? Are they courageous enough to say how they really feel, regardless of public opinion?

As a new believer, I was highly susceptible to the impressions trap. I held my pastor and other Christian authority figures in excessively high regard. After the pastor at my sister's church admitted to sexual misconduct with some of the young men he mentored, I was devastated and disillusioned. I didn't understand how this could happen to a Christian leader. Without realizing it, I had given these Christian leaders a level of respect and authority in my life that rightly belonged to God alone.

When mentors crash and burn, the people who put them on a pedestal are devastated. They may blame the church or even God for failing them. I certainly understand how easy it is to be deceived and disillusioned. I value honor and believe that God wants us to honor others, but when it goes too far and turns into idolization, it limits what God can do in our lives.

This kind of situation is what led the apostle Paul to warn new believers about the dangers of being starstruck by Christian leaders. After Paul departed following a visit to the church in Corinth, the young believers there were led astray by men who made a great impression but who were more intent on amassing a following than leading the body of Christ with integrity. These men used eloquent speech to separate young believers from their faith and from what they'd been taught by the apostle Paul. This created disputes within the church, with some contending Paul was a lesser leader. When Paul learned of their idolization and arguing, he wrote these words:

> When I came to you, I did not come with eloquence or human wisdom as I proclaimed to you the testimony about God. For I resolved to know nothing while I was with you except Jesus Christ and him crucified. . . . My message and my preaching were not with wise and persuasive words, but with a demonstration of the Spirit's power, so that your faith might not rest on human wisdom,

but on God's power. . . . Do not deceive yourselves. . . . For the wisdom of this world is foolishness in God's sight. . . . So then, no more boasting about human leaders! (1 Corinthians 2:1–5; 3:18–21 NIV)

Paul makes it very clear—anytime we idolize other human beings or allow ourselves to be influenced by a flashy impression rather than demonstrated integrity, we are sure to be led astray. Beware of glamorous heroes. Look at a person's track record before giving them your trust in a mentoring relationship.

Treasure in Jars of Clay

Now that we've considered several qualifications for a potential mentor, I can guess what you may be thinking: *Thanks, Bill, but I don't know anyone like that. I'm not sure if anyone that perfect even exists.* Before you give up entirely on the idea of finding a good mentor, hear me out. Your mentor doesn't have to be perfect. We all make mistakes, and we all have flaws—mentors included. So don't look for perfect people. Instead, look for those who aren't afraid to admit their flaws. It's like psychologist Dr. Phil McGraw often says: "You have to own it."

The Bible includes stories of many heroes in the faith but never paints them as perfect. Every single one of them had flaws.

Hero	Flaw
Abraham	Lied to Abimelech; tried to provide his own heir through Hagar instead of waiting on God
Sarah	Doubted God could give her a son in old age
Jacob	Deceived his father, Isaac
Moses	Disobeyed God's command in his anger

Hero	Flaw
Miriam	Questioned God's anointed leader
Rahab	Was a prostitute
Gideon	Was afraid and slow to trust God's plan
David	Was guilty of adultery and murder
Elijah	Wanted to give up and die
Peter	Denied Christ three times
Saul (Paul)	Persecuted Christians

Thousands of years after they walked the earth, these flawed heroes of the faith still inspire and instruct God's people today. Why? Because we can relate to them in their weaknesses and brokenness, and we are encouraged by the way God used them in spite of their failures.

I know that I can identify with them because of my own flaws. I have often wished I had been saved at an earlier age so I could rewrite the mistakes I made growing up. In the early days of my ministry, I didn't speak much about my past. In fact, I had been a pastor for eight years before I shared the complete details of my salvation experience publicly. I felt too ashamed. I didn't want to be one of those people who glamorized a wild life. I had lived every day since my salvation thanking God for my deliverance but always secretly fearing that if all of my past were known, it might be a stumbling block to someone who would consider me unfit for ministry.

One Sunday as I was preaching, I noticed a man in the front row rapidly taking notes. I just assumed he was getting something of value from the message. He approached me after the service and introduced himself—Skip Connett, reporter for the local newspaper. The rapid growth of our church had initially attracted his attention, but as he continued to research me as well as the church, what he discovered about my past made for an even bigger story. He informed me that what he'd discovered would be published the following Sunday.

I felt sick inside. What would our people think if they knew their pastor had lived so aimlessly? They knew about some of my past, but Connett had it *all* in his notes. This was going to be salacious reading for inquiring minds. But when he asked to interview me, I decided to be as honest and forthcoming as I could be. I answered every question truthfully and gave him details that even he hadn't found in his research. And then I prayed: "God, You knew beforehand that this day was coming. I'm going to trust You through this revelation to the public."

I felt that our church people deserved to hear about the details of my past directly from me rather than the newspaper. So on Sunday morning, the day the article was published, I stood at the front of the church and shared my whole story. To my total surprise, people responded not with judgment but with praise to God for His mercy. It gave them hope! After hearing about the failures and bad choices I'd made, many felt they could identify with me. And I felt both accepted and more deeply connected to the people I served because they didn't put me on a pedestal. Instead, they affirmed the fact that we were all sinners and that God loved us regardless of how far we'd once been from Him. People who had almost given up hope that their spouses, children, or friends would ever change and find God were encouraged. My story renewed their hopes that a breakthrough for their loved ones was still possible.

God really does use flawed people. As the Bible says, "But we have this treasure in jars of clay to show that this all-surpassing power is from God and not from us" (2 Cor. 4:7 NIV). The *treasure* is the message of the gospel, and the *jars of clay* are you and me, cracked and flawed as we may be. Your potential mentors will have flaws, too. That's not necessarily a bad thing. In fact, the humility and insights they've gained from their failures may make them even better qualified to guide you. I know I feel more compassion and less judgment toward others because of my past and have a better understanding of how to steer others away from a similar path. If the people you're considering as mentors are open about their mistakes without being proud of them, they may be exactly what you need.

Seek Wisdom

We've covered a lot of territory about how to be wise in selecting a mentor for your journey into a better future. However, it's important to remember that the wisdom of men and women will take you only so far. As you apply the principles you've learned in this chapter, filter them through the ultimate source of knowledge and wisdom: God. He is always the final check on your potential mentors and the guidance they offer.

Solomon, son of King David, was famous for his wisdom. He did not come to it through knowledge and experience alone. Early in his reign as king, Solomon was visited by God.

In that night God appeared to Solomon and said to him, "Ask what I shall give you." Solomon said to God, "You have dealt with my father David with great lovingkindness, and have made me king in his place. Now, O LORD God, Your promise to my father David is fulfilled, for You have made me king over a people as numerous as the dust of the earth. Give me now wisdom and knowledge, that I may go out and come in before this people, for who can rule this great people of Yours?" God said to Solomon, "Because you had this in mind, and did not ask for riches, wealth or honor, or the life of those who hate you, nor have you even asked for long life, but you have asked for yourself wisdom and knowledge that you may rule My people over whom I have made you king, wisdom and knowledge have been granted to you. And I will give you riches and wealth and honor, such as none of the kings who were before you has possessed nor those who will come after you." (2 Chronicles 1:7–12)

Do you see how pleased God was with Solomon's request? He loves it when we come to Him for help. The promise of Scripture is that wisdom is always just a prayer away: "If any of you lacks wisdom, you should ask God, who gives generously to all without finding fault, and it will be given to you" (James 1:5 NIV).

Mentors can be a tremendous aid in the lifelong adventure we call learning. Our quest for guidance must always begin and end, however, with the One who is the source of all wisdom.

Insights for Inspiration

- One of the best ways to learn is to "go to school on another man's shot."
- Be impressed by integrity rather than impressions.
- Look for godly qualities and character in your mentors, but don't expect them to be perfect.

Verse to Review

"Instruct the wise, and they will be even wiser. Teach the righteous, and they will learn even more" (Prov. 9:9 NLT).

Getting Personal

- Briefly identify one or two people you admire and respect. What specific character traits do you admire most about them?
- Of the four qualities a good mentor should have, which is most important to you? Why?
- What issue or questions would you most like to work through with a mentor? How do you hope a mentor might be able to help you?

10

Coping with Critics

It is only at the tree loaded with
fruit that men throw stones.
Charles H. Spurgeon

We've already talked about crabs and the amazing transformations they undergo when they molt. But they're interesting creatures in another way, too. If you've ever been crabbing, you might know what I mean. As long as you catch more than one crab, you don't need a lid for your bucket. You can leave the top wide open and the crabs won't escape.

Here's the reason. Every time one crab starts to crawl out of the bucket, the others pull it back in. They're comfortable as long as everyone's in the bucket. But if one starts to climb upward, the others whip out their claws. Instead of following the adventurous crab to freedom, jealousy drives the others to pull the escapee back down. Little do these crabs know that their comfort zone is really a danger zone. They're all headed for the same place—the big boiling pot! If only they realized they were as good as dead in the bucket, they might be willing to help each other out instead of pulling each other down.

Something similar happens to you and me. When we start to crawl out of our old way of life, it won't be long until we meet with some kind of resistance. Try to break through to a new way of life and the "crabs" will soon stretch out their claws to pull you back down. Growth and success prompt jealousy. Everyone wants to be successful, but few want *you* to be successful.

I discovered this crab dynamic when I began pastoring at Cascade Hills. With just thirty-two members, our church wasn't a threat to anyone. You might say we were a little church in a big bucket. For years, I attended a weekly luncheon for area pastors and was treated kindly by most of them. Each year when they gave out a plaque to recognize church growth, I always celebrated with the pastors who were honored. When our church first experienced a bit of growth, people patted me on the back and said, "Good job," but it was a little condescending—it was clear they didn't expect much from me or from the church.

But when the number of our baptisms and church membership started to explode, everything changed. Now when I attended a luncheon I was treated like I had leprosy. One week when I sat down at a table with seven other pastors, they all looked at each other, nodded their heads, got up, and moved to another table. Feeling confused, rejected, and hurt, I sat alone through the entire lunch. *What happened?*

Later, one pastor said to me, "You may have had some quick success, but God will never bless someone like you with a long-term, successful ministry." Another pastor said, "You've got to be doing something wrong. You must be taking shortcuts to make your church grow so fast."

I was hurt and confused by their comments and wondered why anyone would jump to such negative conclusions about our growth. However, the more I examined the situation as well as my own motives, the more I realized it wasn't what I was doing *wrong* but what I was doing *right* that provoked the criticism. The other pastors were jealous.

I had to make a choice. Either I could let people like these pastors pull me back into the bucket of their comfort zone, or I could keep climbing. I decided to stay the course. I wasn't going to remain stagnant or compromise my calling to avoid criticism and win acceptance. My goal was to do something of value and significance.

As you start to climb out of the bucket in your own life, be prepared. Sooner or later, the crabs around you will notice and do anything to pull you down. And you don't really know who the crabs in your life are until you start to climb. They might say things like, "You've changed," meaning that the change is something they disapprove of. Some crabs get very uncomfortable when you take steps to advance your personal journey. Jealous people get nervous whenever you start to change and grow. They would rather you not break out because it might make them look bad or remind them of their unwillingness to change. Unfortunately, this often prevents talented people from reaching their potential. They get halfway out of the bucket and then give up because they can't handle the criticism. Those same talented people never understand why people with fewer gifts or skills soon surpass them. Gifts and skills take a person only so far. What makes the difference at the highest levels is not just skills but will—a will that refuses to be discouraged or distracted by critics.

The Betrayal Factor

The more progress and growth you experience, the more jealousy you're likely to encounter. We all experience jealousy at some point in our lives, but critics are often consumed by it.

Jealousy has been described as "resentment against a rival" and "an unhappy or angry feeling of wanting to have what someone else has." It springs from focusing on others and what they possess instead of focusing on God and what He's given us. It's an attitude that's obsessed with self. The more people dwell on what they lack, the stronger their feelings of jealousy grow and the more miserable they become: "A heart at peace gives life to the body, but envy rots the bones" (Prov. 14:30 NIV). If critics see you moving forward in life, they may project their misery onto you. Your achievements will always test both you and the people around you.

Once, a man who'd been criticized for buying a new house asked me, "What's the difference between enjoying God's blessings and being materialistic?"

"The difference," I explained, "has to do with who has the new house. When your critics have a new house, they say, 'God blessed us.' But if you have a new house, you're being materialistic."

The Bible tells us, "Rejoice with those who rejoice, and weep with those who weep" (Rom. 12:15). Many people have it backward—they rejoice with those who weep, and weep with those who rejoice. If you were to reach all your goals, would your friends rejoice?

Of course, many people who are jealous don't even realize it. Your critics certainly won't speak up and admit that they are jealous. Instead, they might clothe it in deep concern. When you're blessed, instead of rejoicing with you, they'll rush in to say, "Stay humble." Jealous people use the "stay humble" card a lot, but when they do, they're saying more about themselves than you. True friends always rejoice in your progress and your blessings.

Your friends will be watching as you pursue God's vision for your life. The closer you get to that vision, the greater their temptation to give in to jealousy. When jealousy takes over, it typically rears its head over one of the following:

- *Possessions*: "I want what they have." Your vision might include hosting youth groups in your home. But if you buy a big-screen TV or stereo system to make your home more appealing for those youth, your critics may not like it.

- *Positions*: "I want to be where they are." The pastor at your church sees your potential as a worship leader and promotes you—be prepared to hear whispers behind your back.

- *Privileges*: "I want to do what they get to do." The head of the environmental company where you work asks you to join the advance travel team that will prepare for an upcoming conference in Europe. Don't expect everyone in the office to be happy about it.

- *Progress*: "I want to achieve what they've achieved." You change your marketing approach, become more open and honest, and double your sales. You may be shunned by colleagues because of it.

- *People*: "I want to be who they are." As you share your vision for creating a foundation for abused children, almost everyone in your circle gets more and more excited about it and you. The people who don't may very well be jealous.

All too often, the jealousy your critics experience over your progress will move beyond a feeling into something more. They will tend to lash out with their words or actions. The result is betrayal.

Betrayal by Words

The apostle James wrote, "The tongue is a small part of the body, and yet it boasts of great things. . . . See how great a forest is set aflame by such a small fire!" (James 3:5). We might think that the devastating power of the tongue would make it easy to recognize, but betrayal by the tongue is often subtle. It begins with a jealous, competitive spirit that lays seeds of doubt about you in the minds of others. People might whisper, "I wonder where he got the money to pay for that," or "I don't know what they see in her." There is little you can do to prevent it. Just as jealous crabs are relentless in their attempts to pull down any climbers, jealous critics will take every opportunity to degrade your reputation. Dr. Phil McGraw describes such people this way: "To your face, they profess their undying loyalty to you. Behind your back, they're poisoning the well."[1] Nothing hurts as much as being rejected or betrayed by a close friend. It's the hardest emotional price I've ever had to pay for growth.

Betrayal by Actions

Some people may become so consumed with jealousy over positive changes in your life that they move swiftly from words to action. It might be a seemingly small or passive action such as failing to pass along important information about the committee meeting next week. Or it might be an extreme action, as was the case with King Saul and David.

As the first king of Israel, Saul had anything he wanted at his command—power, wealth, and privileges. There wasn't anything he needed to be afraid of. Yet he felt threatened by a teenage shepherd boy. Saul just couldn't handle David's rising popularity.

After David defeated Goliath, the women of Israel sang: "Saul has slain his thousands, and David his ten thousands" (1 Sam. 18:7). For Saul, what started out as irritation over the words of a song eventually led to attempted murder. Gone unchecked, jealousy grows until it controls people, and they will justify almost any action in an effort to put you down. And what the jealous person fails to realize is how much their jealousy is costing them. Those who indulge jealousy incur at least three significant losses.

- *They lose peace.* "Saul became very angry, for this saying displeased him" (1 Sam. 18:8). Saul could not handle the admiration and attention David received.

- *They lose focus.* "Saul looked at David with suspicion from that day on" (1 Sam. 18:9). Saul kept track of David, wanting to hear reports of him at all times. He spent the rest of his days obsessed with watching David rather than leading his people.

- *They lose control.* "Saul hurled the spear for he thought, 'I will pin David to the wall'" (1 Sam. 18:11). Saul's jealousy finally exploded in his attempt to kill David. Uncontrollable rage guided his actions from that day on.

Plenty of people in your circle will continue to love, support, encourage, and guide you when you begin stepping into your destiny. And hopefully none of them will try to kill you! But jealousy is a powerful emotion that we all deal with at one point or another. A little grace on your part toward those who are struggling with your growth and progress may help them overcome their envy. That doesn't mean compromising your growth, but it might mean showing compassion to friends who still have some growing to do themselves.

Handling Your Critics

So what should you do if you find yourself surrounded by critics or jealous friends? You can start by being encouraged. Criticism and jealousy are often indicators that you're growing and making progress. Plus, persevering through these obstacles not only strengthens your character but also may be the very path that leads to your destiny. Consider the outcome for three men in the Bible who were betrayed by close friends:

- Joseph, betrayed by his own brothers and sold into slavery, became the second most powerful man in the world (Genesis 41).

- Moses, betrayed by a relative from his tribe and two hundred fifty other men of "renown," became the only man ever to encounter Jehovah God face-to-face (Deut. 34:10).

- Jesus, betrayed by one of His chosen disciples, became the Savior of the world and is now seated at the right hand of God the Father (Phil. 2:7–11).

Do you see how God used every betrayal and hardship to prepare each one for his destiny? If you don't allow your critics and betrayers to defeat you, chances are good that you'll experience the same. Instead of a brick wall of opposition, your critics may actually be the door that leads where God wants you to be. One time my wife had a critic who just would not let her jealousy die. A wise, godly friend said to her, "Don't let it bother you. When she talks about you, she's giving someone else a break."

In addition to being encouraged, you can take several other practical steps to keep your critics from derailing your ride to your destiny. You can inspect yourself, ignore your critics, stand up to your critics, close the door to critics, and keep clear relational boundaries to avoid critics.

Inspect yourself. Not all criticism is bad. Sometimes it can help you recognize your faults. The Bible tells us, "Faithful are the wounds of a friend, but deceitful are the kisses of an enemy" (Prov. 27:6). Ask yourself: "Is there any truth to this criticism?" Then ask a trusted friend or mentor the same question. If you discern that there is any truth to it, own up to it and address it.

Ignore your critics. Take the advice of the proverb: "Make no friendship with an angry man . . . lest thou learn his ways, and get a snare to thy soul" (Prov. 22:24–25 KJV). The greatest danger in handling critics is becoming like them. Don't waste your time trying to put out fires all the time. You'll wear yourself out and lose your focus. Jesus called it throwing "your pearls before swine" (Matt. 7:6). Often your best response is simply to continue doing what God has called you to do.

When the prophet Nehemiah was rebuilding the wall around Jerusalem, his critics wanted to meet with him to discuss their differences. But Nehemiah knew it was a trap—they intended to harm him to keep him from rebuilding the wall. He replied, "I am doing a great work and I cannot come down. Why should the work stop while I leave it and come down to you?" (Neh. 6:3). He rejected their requests five times and completed the entire wall in just fifty-two days (Neh. 6:15). His critics were silenced for good. Had Nehemiah wasted his time trying to answer them, he would have delayed and sacrificed the work God had called him to.

Stand up to your critics. If you think this sounds like the opposite of the advice above, you're right. There will be times when simply ignoring your critics either is not an option or is unwise. Constant criticism from a parent, for example, may create a toxic atmosphere for your spouse and kids. In that case, you need to do something about the situation for the sake of your family. Prayer and wisdom will guide you in knowing when you must stand up to your detractors.

Standing up to your critics doesn't mean going on the offensive, returning insult with insult, or blowing up in anger. Instead, plan ahead of time what you want to say and sit down with your critic privately. Be calm but firm as you deliver your message. If it's a parent, let him or her know that whatever their opinion, things have to change or you'll be forced to put an end to family visits.

It takes courage to confront your critics, but if you commit to honor God in the way you approach them, He will always stand with you.

Close the door to critics. When someone comes to me and says, "What do you think about John?" I know immediately that they are seeking permission to say something negative about John. I enjoy watching them stammer when I say something like, "I love John. He is one of my best buddies. Now, what was it you wanted to tell me about John?" Suddenly, they have nothing more to say.

I'm leery of such folks because I've learned when people talk about someone else to you, they'll talk about you to someone else. When you're around people like that, it's best to close the door on them by keeping your mouth shut.

Keep clear relational boundaries to avoid critics. I have developed rings of intimacy in my life and relationships. Imagine a series of three concentric circles or rings—that's my relational world. At the very center is the deepest level of intimacy, which is limited to my family members. This is where I have the freedom and safety to be most vulnerable. In the next ring out is what I sometimes refer to as my inner circle—a few close friends I know I can trust to rejoice with me in blessings and weep with me in failures. No critics allowed. In the outer ring are people with whom I have more casual relationships. I'm open to potentially developing deeper levels of trust with them, but until that happens, I don't allow them into my inner circle.

The only way someone can move from the outer ring to my inner circle is through the tests of time and loyalty. Anyone can sustain the appearance of loyalty for a few days or weeks. The people who are truly devoted to you, however, will still be on your side months and years later. They will have had opportunities to join your critics or stand on the sidelines when you needed help but will instead have stepped forward to offer their encouragement, resources, and sage advice. That's why I recommend being cautious of people who try to move quickly into your intimate circle. They have not been tested. Those who enter quickly usually leave quickly. It's better to be lonely than surrounded by a company of critics.

I hope these practical steps give you options for how to deal with jealous critics. Their presence may annoy and even hurt you, but they also may be an indication that you are headed in exactly the right direction. Continue to talk to God about your detractors, and I'm confident He'll guide you to the proper response.

Rising from the Bottom of the Bucket

Criticism is sometimes the price we pay for breaking free of our old life and daring to discover a better future. You can let it hinder you or choose to reach higher. God didn't design you to live at the bottom of a bucket. When our friends the crabs begin to break out of their shells, they find the process scary and painful. Yet the price they pay is far less than the price they would pay for staying in the shell—death by suffocation. H. Jackson Brown, author of *Life's Little Instruction Book*, puts it this way:

You pay a price for getting stronger.

    You pay a price for getting faster.

    You pay a price for jumping higher.

    [But also] you pay a price for staying just the same.[2]

As you begin to break free, critics will inevitably show up. You get to choose how you respond to their jealousy. You can let it hinder you or choose to use it as motivation to keep reaching for your dreams. When adversity comes, keep moving forward.

Insights for Inspiration

- Jealous people feel threatened by change and growth in others.

- True friends always rejoice in your growth, achievements, and blessings.

- Criticism is the price we pay for breaking free of our old life.

Verse to Review

*"Do not answer a fool according to his folly,
or you will also be like him"* (Prov. 26:4).

Getting Personal

- When have critics tried to keep you from "climbing out of the bucket"? What do you think motivated their resistance?

- Do you ever avoid change because you fear the criticism of others?

- Which of the steps for handling critics might you use to deal with the critics in your life right now?

The Way Up Is Down

A man who is at the top is a man who has
the habit of getting to the bottom.
Joseph E. Rogers

Early in my ministry, I learned very quickly that I would never get anywhere by trying to exalt myself. If I tried to promote myself, I failed. If I tried to do things in my own power, I failed. Remember that first time I got up to preach in church? I was so scared that I prayed all through the night before. Then my terror turned to amazement when people actually came to Christ in response to my bungling attempt at a sermon. I remember thinking later, *That wasn't so bad, after all. Just read a verse and say something about it and people will want to know Jesus.*

The next time I was asked to preach, I didn't spend as much time in prayer or preparation because I was "experienced." I'm sure my second message wasn't any worse than my first—in fact, it had to be better. But this time, nothing happened. At the end, no one came up wanting to know Jesus. That's when I realized that without God I could do nothing. I decided that day that I would never stand up before people without first going down on my knees in God's presence. To this day, I still spend time with God in private before I ever get up to preach. I trust that if I humble myself before God, He will lift me up.

Humility Lessons

Humility is perhaps the most essential quality you need in order to reach your destiny. Andrew Murray defined humility as the ability "to be at rest when nobody praises me and when I am blamed or despised."[1] I like his definition because it so readily applies to those who seek to make a change and break out of old patterns. If we're rooted in humility, no one else's applause or criticism can throw us off course. That's the pathway to lasting change.

As I mentioned in the last chapter, early in my ministry career, I had to learn to be at peace without the support of my peers. I was shunned by some pastors just because I was different. When I was left alone at the pastors' luncheon, that rejection hurt. Yet I knew I had to choose between their acceptance and what I considered my calling. If I had listened to my insecurities and chased after their praise, I wouldn't have the ministry or the freedom I have today.

I certainly don't claim to be an expert on humility. I think once you've become aware of your humility you've pretty much lost it. I once heard of a man who was proud of being humble. The church gave him a ribbon for exemplifying humility; then the elders took it away from him when he wore it. When it comes to humility, I still have a lot to learn. Life, in fact, seems to be one long lesson in humility. I can just about guarantee that if you think you've got everything figured out and under control one minute, the next will show you how wrong you are.

I was reminded of that truth during a difficult period that began in the Christmas season of 2006. Membership at our church was growing rapidly, we were initiating new programs, and everything seemed to be going great. I was in New York with our media team when a staff member tried to use the church credit card to pay the bill at our hotel. The card was rejected, so I put everyone's expenses on my personal credit card. When I was on the phone a few hours later with our church's chief financial officer back home, I mentioned the card issue. "I'll get it fixed," she said. "Don't worry about it."

Still, the incident nagged at me. Something didn't seem right. When I got back to Columbus, I asked our financial officer—I'll call her Lisa—to come into my office. "How are things financially with the church?" I asked.

Before she could respond, we were interrupted by another staff member. Standing with her was a technician from Georgia Power. "We're going to have to cut off the lights at the church," he said.

"Pardon me?" I said. As we were trying to figure things out with the technician, we had yet another visitor. This one was from the IRS. He said we hadn't been paying our payroll taxes and they wanted to see the books.

After our visitors left, I turned back to Lisa. "You need to tell me the truth," I said. "What in the world is going on?"

Lisa got up, walked to her office, then returned with a cardboard box filled with papers. "These bills have not been paid," she said, an embarrassed look on her face. While I was trying to get my head around the fact that this box was spilling over with unpaid bills, she said, "I'll go get the other box."

My heart hit the floor.

Lisa had been handling the books for the church's finances, as well as my family's finances, for nearly twenty years. But when the church started growing so quickly, she got behind on paying the bills. She also allowed some of the staff to spend funds without getting approval. She valued those relationships and enjoyed being in a position to help her colleagues.

Instead of telling anyone about the church's financial problems, Lisa tried to resolve them herself. The situation grew out of control. Lisa was a longtime friend whom I loved and trusted implicitly. I knew she never would have intentionally hurt me or the church, but she'd slowly gotten in over her head. None of us realized it until it was too late.

I was stunned by the number of bills in those two cardboard boxes. When we first added them up, we were staring at $755,000 in debt. Later, we learned that the debt was actually more than a million dollars. I believed that our church and my ministry were finished. I never thought this was how it would end.

When I got home that day, I didn't go into the house. I walked straight down to the lake at the edge of our property. "God," I prayed, "I'm sorry. I'm the pastor and I'm responsible for this. I never meant to cause harm to Your name. I don't want any creditors to say we've defrauded them. I don't know how or when, but I'll pay back every cent. I repent. I'll do whatever it takes to turn this around."

I told our staff what was happening, but I decided not to tell the congregation. Debbie and I then used everything we'd saved and invested over the previous thirty years to start paying off the bills. I went personally to all the local people we owed money to and said, "I want to apologize to you. Here's a check to cover these debts in full."

Several people on our staff, including some Debbie and I counted as close friends, decided we were a sinking ship and jumped swiftly to jobs at other churches. That hurt, and only added to our problems. It was a hard, dark season. After Debbie and I depleted everything we had, our home was all that was left. We prepared to sell it. We were broke. There is nothing quite as humbling as thinking you have life under control and then suddenly discovering that you're about to lose everything.

Except it wasn't everything. As deep as the losses were, I still had the unconditional love and support of Debbie, my three boys, and their wives. I also had the backing of our remaining staff and friends, some of whom surprised and touched me with their help when they discovered what was happening. Most importantly, I still had God. I was reminded once again that I could accomplish nothing without His help. I prayed and prayed and felt closer to Him than ever. It was a humble place to be—which was also the best place I could possibly be.

From that position of humble submission, I saw God begin to work.

Donations began pouring in, many of them from people who didn't even know about our need. Every dollar that came in was applied to the debt. I was learning that the emptier I was before God each day, the more He kept sending the resources we needed. Within a year, our debt was paid in full.

I waited a full year after the crisis before I told the congregation what had happened. I felt it was my mess and that I was the one who needed to take responsibility for cleaning it up. Little did I know how quickly God would show us grace. Many people came up to me after hearing what had happened and said, "If I'd only known, I would have helped." One friend was actually frustrated with me and said, "I would have given you the entire amount if you'd called me." I knew that he could and would have, but I felt that wouldn't have been right—it was my responsibility to deal with.

We learned many things from that experience, not the least of which was to put systems and professionals in place to avoid ever going down that road again. Today, the church is in a much stronger position financially. What began as a disaster became an occasion for the display of God's miraculous power and the love of so many people around me. Three years later, Debbie and I witnessed more miracles that restored our personal finances well beyond what we'd given away. For me, the entire experience was a breakthrough to a deeper faith and confirmation that nothing can hold us back from our destiny if we are willing to stay humble and depend on God no matter what.

Although life continually gives us opportunities to stay humble, some of us don't get the message. We forget that God did not put us on this planet to be served, but to serve.

Serving Instead of Impressing

I heard about a young man who was scheduled to give the valedictorian's speech at his commencement. He couldn't wait to show off his oratory skills to his fellow graduates. He strutted up to the platform and launched into his speech, feeling like a self-confident expert who would certainly impress the crowd. However, a few moments into his speech, he began to lose the flow. His words started running together, and he realized when he looked out at his peers that they seemed more baffled than impressed. "I'm sorry," he said, his face red with shame. Then he collected his notes, hung his head, and slumped to the edge of the stage.

The crowd was silent and no one moved. As the young man passed by, the commencement speaker caught his arm. Gently pulling him close, he gave the young man a lesson to remember. "Son," he said, "if you had gone up to the podium like you came down, you could have come down like you went up." That was wise advice.

Trying to impress others to win recognition just isn't that important. People who value what others think love to try to impress because it makes them feel important. But true significance doesn't come from making a flashy impression; it comes from humbly doing something of value.

Jesus is the Son of God, but when He was on earth He was more interested in serving than in impressing people. At the pinnacle of Jesus' ministry, He reached for a towel and washed the disciples' feet. On the night before His crucifixion, Jesus could have spent His time at the Last Supper describing His impending glory—how He would soon ascend to heaven and sit at God's right hand. Instead, the Son of God got down on His hands and knees and did the work of a servant.

Ironically, it was during that same Passover supper that the disciples argued over who should be greatest among them. Jesus had just finished showing and telling them that "whoever wishes to become great among you shall be your servant; and whoever wishes to be first among you shall be slave of all" (Mark 10:43–44). But they weren't interested in taking on the job of the slave; they wanted to be exalted. Fortunately, Jesus willingly accepted the job He was called to do. "The Son of Man," He said, "did not come to be served, but to serve, and to give His life a ransom for many" (Mark 10:45). The next day He fulfilled His calling by dying on the cross to pay the penalty for our sin.

If we consider ourselves above humble service, chances are good we'll miss our calling. God's grand plan for each of us is guaranteed to include serving others, but we'll miss it if our attitude lacks humility. Anyone who is too big for a little job is really too little for a big job. It's usually right about the time that we've gotten comfortable with our current level of growth or achievement that God calls us to step out, take a risk, and move toward our future. Those new assignments may not appear to be important or good career moves at first, but when coupled with a desire to do God's will, they inevitably take us farther down the road to our destiny.

Here's one example of what I mean by taking on a new assignment that doesn't initially appear important. When I look back, I realize that every job I ever had in ministry began with a pay cut. Every new venture to which God called me initially looked like a step backward. That's humbling! But after I trusted Him and took the risk, I also realized that He always knew what He was doing. If we limit ourselves by only accepting opportunities that are "bigger and better," we might well miss out on God's best. Difference-makers are willing to go wherever God calls them because they know that their significance is in God's hands. They are willing to accept what some might consider a lowly position because they know they are highly valued in their Father's eyes.

To better understand how humility is crucial to our destiny, consider the linguistic roots of the word itself. The word *humility* originates from the Latin root word *homo*, meaning "man." This origin gives humility a sense of "being common" or "not giving dignity to oneself." When it later evolved into the word *humilis,* it meant "of the ground" or "of the earth." *Humilis* began to be used as a term meaning "to acknowledge oneself as another's servant." Which takes us right back to the issue of finding our significance in God and our service to Him. There's a reason those who break out of their old lives aren't afraid of taking whatever assignment God gives them. It's because they're humble enough to know that the only recognition that really matters comes from God, not people. To be humble is to see ourselves as we are, common men and women, joyfully employed in God's service.

One of my favorite people is former Columbus High School baseball coach Bobby Howard. Bobby is a living legend with over nine hundred wins in his career and twelve state championships. ESPN and *Sports Illustrated* have both recognized him as "Coach of the Year." Bobby's been a big part of helping several players make it to the major leagues, including Hall of Famer Frank Thomas, who recognized Coach Howard in his acceptance speech at Cooperstown in 2014.

While his competitive spirit and emphasis on excellence are unmatched, it's Coach Howard's humility that sets him apart from the pack. I've watched him stop in the middle of a playoff game to help an elderly woman find a good seat so she could watch her grandson play. He'll pause and listen to every parent who tells him that one day their child will be the best he'll ever coach, and he always agrees with them. Bobby walks through a crowd with class. He pauses to laugh with those who are happy, says an encouraging word to those in need, and listens politely as people who've never played the game tell him how to coach. He always reminds me how humility looks on a winner.

In the world of high school baseball, Bobby Howard has been one of America's greats. He found his life calling and never wavered from it. He never let success go to his head. Over the years, he's influenced countless young men for the better because he consistently maintained a humble spirit.

If we are going to find our calling and enjoy the influence God has designed us for, we also must develop humility. But to learn how to develop genuine humility, we need to do a heart check.

A Heart Condition

Sometimes the best way to understand something is to contrast it with what it is *not*. Here are three common misconceptions about humility that describe what it is and is not.

***Humility is not bad posture; humility is *a posture of the heart.** It's not hanging your head low, slouching, or being afraid to look somebody in the eye. Humility cannot be judged by how you dress or present yourself to others. The Bible tells us, "People look at the outside of a person, but the LORD looks at the heart" (1 Sam. 16:7 NCV).

I heard a story about a rabbi who humbled himself in preparation for the Day of Atonement. He paraded around, beating his chest and shouting, "I am nothing. I am nothing." The cantor saw him and followed the example of his rabbi. So the two of them marched through the synagogue demonstrating their humility. The janitor also witnessed this ritual and was reminded of his own sinfulness. He too began to beat his chest and cry, "I am nothing. I am nothing." When the rabbi heard the janitor, he turned smugly to the cantor and said, "Look who thinks he's nothing."

We are not humble because we think we are humble, say we are humble, or hang our heads like we're humble. Humility is not a condition of appearance; it's a condition of the heart. Actually, it's a broken heart condition. Just as the crab must be broken before it can grow outside of its shell, you and I have to be broken before we can grow. Brokenness is important because it teaches us humility. It's what makes us completely dependent on God.

Think of it this way. When the physical heart that beats in your chest is damaged and sometimes fails to send the electrical impulses that keep it beating, doctors often implant an artificial pacemaker. The job of the pacemaker is to send timed electric shocks to the heart in place of the impulses to keep the heart beating regularly and sustain life.

When our spiritual heart is damaged, there is room for God to move in as our Pacemaker. His will is implanted in our heart. His heartbeat becomes our heartbeat, and our life becomes dependent on Him. Just as a heart that isn't broken physically doesn't need a pacemaker, a heart that isn't broken spiritually doesn't need God. That's the beauty of humility. Humility creates a need for us to be dependent on God, which enables Him to point us toward His plan for our future.

Humility is not self-effacement; humility is finding significance in God. Some people are so insecure that they will do anything for attention, even put themselves down. Have you ever been around people who always belittle themselves just to get you to affirm them by saying, "That's not true"? One lady got so tired of hearing her husband cut himself down in order to get her praise that she was finally honest with him and said, "Don't be so humble—you're not that great!" C. S. Lewis must have been tired of dealing with one of these humble people when he said, "A man is never so proud as when striking an attitude of humility."[2] Truly humble people don't have to go around telling you how worthless or humble they are.

The problem with the husband is that his focus remained on himself. It's when we keep our eyes on God that we begin to understand our place in creation. That is the paradox—recognizing both how small and unworthy we are compared to the vastness of the universe and yet how infinitely loved and valuable we are to a God who sent His Son to die for us and has a plan and purpose for our future.

Humility is not the opposite of pride; humility is confidence in God. Sometimes good people are accused of not being humble because they are confident or bold. But humility is not a lack of confidence. To be prideful is to have confidence in oneself. To be humble is to have confidence in God. In this regard, I believe in practicing the under-wear principle: Humility is like underwear—essential but indecent if it shows.

Humility doesn't draw attention to itself. Genuine humility comes from seeing yourself before God. Clergyman Phillips Brooks said, "The true way to be humble is not to stoop until you are smaller than your-self, but to stand at your real height against some higher nature that will show you what the real smallness of your greatness is."[3] The prophet Micah wrote, "And what does the LORD require of you but to do justice, to love kindness, and to walk humbly with your God?" (Micah 6:8). Notice that this verse does not say "be humble" or "walk humbly," but "walk humbly with your God." You cannot make yourself humble on your own. Humility is the result of walking daily in the presence of God. When you view yourself in the light of God's presence, you cannot help but be humbled—or be confident in Him—because He is so awesome.

These three examples of what humility is not and what it is—as well as the "symptoms" that follow—should give you a basis for doing your own periodic heart check. Though it's easy to drift away from a humble attitude, if you continue to depend on God to guide you, chances are good you'll remain humble and stay on course to discover your destiny.

Are You Showing Symptoms?

Discovering and living into your best future depends on developing a sincere humility. The challenge is that when we make an effort to be humble, we run the risk of developing false humility instead. However, there are a few "symptoms" we can look for to assess how we're doing when it comes to living an authentically humble life. They include a servant attitude, willingness to forgive, approachability, gratitude, and humility in good times.

Servant Attitude

A servant attitude is almost always a symptom of the genuinely humble heart. No one modeled this better than Jesus when He washed His disciples' feet. Obviously, it should have been the other way around. Jesus did this because He wanted to get across an important message: "If I then, the Lord and the Teacher, washed your feet, you also ought to wash one another's feet. For I gave you an example that you also should do as I did to you" (John 13:14–15). Jesus commanded us to follow His example of serving others.

Genuine humility isn't self-centered; it's centered on serving others. Are your dreams drawing you closer to having a servant's heart or pulling you farther away? Does the path you're taking to get there help or hurt others? I often find that when things start to become all about me, it's time to make a U-turn because I'm heading in the wrong direction. If your dream will benefit others in a tangible way, it's much more likely to be part of your destiny.

Willingness to Forgive

The true condition of your heart is seen in the way you treat people who have hurt you. When you are humbly mindful of your own shortcomings, it's easier to offer forgiveness. Pride, on the other hand, tends to prevent us from forgiving or forgetting faults. This is a dangerous place to be, because an unforgiving heart ultimately brings bitterness. Simply put, forgiveness is the only way to travel light, without the baggage that bitterness brings.

The Bible makes clear what our approach should be: "Let all bitterness and wrath and anger and clamor and slander be put away from you, along with all malice. Be kind to one another, tender-hearted, forgiving each other, just as God in Christ also has forgiven you" (Eph. 4:31–32).

How willing are you to forgive those who have wronged you? Maybe offering forgiveness is the last obstacle you need to remove so you can step toward your dreams. I know, I know. If I only knew what they did to you, I would understand why you're not willing to go there. Yet Jesus was asked how many times He should offer forgiveness to someone who continued to wrong Him, and He answered, "Seventy times seven" (Matt. 18:22). That's a lot of forgiveness, friend.

Approachability

How approachable we are says a lot about us. Do we treat all people as equally important and accept them as they are? Or do we try to intimidate others as a means of establishing our position and power? When the disciples believed little children were bothering Jesus and tried to send them away, Jesus said, "Permit the children to come to Me; do not hinder them; for the kingdom of God belongs to such as these" (Mark 10:14). He was as welcoming and approachable to little children as He was to those in positions of influence and authority.

I think I know a little bit of what those little children might have felt when Jesus welcomed them. A couple of times, I've attended ministry conferences and been invited to lunch with people who were very prominent. What I've discovered is that the truly great ones are always approachable and welcoming. They don't talk down to people or play a role to puff up their own importance. On the other hand, the "wannabes" and the "never-will-bes" are more arrogant than approachable. They tend to demand recognition and chase after honor. I soon realized that those who are the most arrogant usually don't have anything to be proud about. That's why they're unapproachable in the first place.

Arrogance doesn't make you great. Approachability is what reveals true greatness. Do others find you accessible, or do they keep their distance because of your arrogance? What if that seemingly insignificant person is the future partner you need to meet so he or she can propel you to your future? It will happen only if you are approachable.

Gratitude

I love how members of the Masai tribe in West Africa show gratitude. They bow, put their foreheads on the ground, and say, "My head is in the dirt."[4] The Masai understand that expressing gratitude is a humble act. To give thanks is to recognize the value and worth of someone else.

The apostle Paul points out that gratitude is a key requirement for living in the will of God. He writes that we must "always giv[e] thanks for all things in the name of our Lord Jesus Christ to God" (Eph. 5:20). The proud always think they deserve better. The humble are grateful for what they have. Saying a heartfelt "thank you"—to God and others—shows humility.

Don't wait, however, until you reach your destiny and fulfill your dreams to be grateful. You've got be grateful where you are now. God is shaping and molding you for the future He's planned for you. A thankful attitude today may be exactly the attitude He's looking for so He can open the door to His purpose for you tomorrow.

Humility in Good Times

All of us have problems in life, and how we respond to our trials is critical. But just as important is how we respond to progress, growth, and success. If you really want to know if people possess true humility, watch how they respond in the good times.

The apostle Peter wrote, "God is opposed to the proud, but gives grace to the humble. Therefore humble yourselves under the mighty hand of God, that He may exalt you at the proper time" (1 Peter 5:5–6). God will not give sustained grace—His favor and blessing—to someone without genuine humility. If you see a formerly struggling and humble person begin to puff up and take their success for granted, it's likely they've wandered off the road toward God's designed future. And the same is true for you and me.

Martin Luther once said, "God creates out of nothing. Therefore, until a man is nothing, God can make nothing out of him."[5] Humility makes us usable. With humility comes teachability, and being teachable makes us available to accomplish God's purposes and to forget our own. We need to remember that if we hope to discover our destiny.

Humble Practices

While considering our symptoms helps us look for evidence of humility, there are four practices we can use that actually foster genuine humility within us. We must keep ourselves in perspective, give praise, and acknowledge the power of God.

Keep Yourself in Perspective

Humility has to do with seeing ourselves rightly. It happens when God opens our eyes and we see the gravity of our sin and His enormous power and love. When Isaiah saw the Lord in all His splendor and glory sitting on the throne, he said, "Woe is me, for I am ruined! Because I am a man of unclean lips" (Isa. 6:5). When we see God for who He is, we learn to see ourselves rightly—how wretched we are compared to His glory and how much we need His power and love.

Pride looks out and focuses on the faults of others. In the process, it blinds us to our own faults. Humility opens our eyes, helping us to look in and face the quiet truth of the heart. As long as you are looking outward at others, you will always be able to find someone whose faults make you look better. But if you are looking at God, you will see your true condition. That's what it means to keep yourself in perspective.

Give Praise—to God and Others

Rather than seeking praise for yourself, make it a habit to give praise. The moment you start thinking you're a virtuous person who deserves recognition is the moment you're vulnerable to being blinded by pride. Someone once asked author and Holocaust survivor Corrie ten Boom how she handled all the praise she received without becoming proud. She answered wisely that she looked at each compliment as a beautiful, long-stemmed flower. She smelled it for a moment and then put it into a vase with the others. Each night, just before going to bed, she took the beautiful bouquet and handed it over to God, saying, "Thank you, Lord, for letting me smell the flowers; they all belong to you."[6]

Proud people are afraid of giving praise to others. They're afraid that shining a light on someone else's accomplishments will somehow take light away from their own. Instead of giving praise and affirmation, they are intentional about withholding it. I love what Abraham Lincoln implied about holding on to praise when he said, "What kills a skunk is the publicity it gives itself."[7] If you withhold praise too long, you start to stink.

Practice giving praise away. When someone pats you on the back for something you did, develop a practice of giving God the praise. Remembering that God is the reason for every good thing in your life and for every good thing you're able to accomplish will keep your pride in check. It's impossible to be proud of something you don't take credit for in the first place.

Acknowledge the Power of God

When you know who you are, you will always marvel at what God can do through you. I'm not impressed with myself because I know me too well. I remember where I came from. Occasionally someone will praise me for the amazing growth of our church, yet when I think about how far our little church has come, it doesn't fill me with pride.

I am humbled that the presence and power of God has taken us this far. In fact, I wonder what God could have done if we'd depended on Him more. I know I am not worthy of our success or responsible for our success. I know me, and I am just not that good. In fact, with each blessing we receive, I still can't help wondering if there's been a mix-up in heaven. The more we're blessed, however, the more it drives us to acknowledge the power of God and to increase our dependence on Him.

You know yourself well, too, don't you? If we're completely honest with ourselves and if humility really *does* become part of our DNA, we have to acknowledge the power of God in our lives. Without it, we would be nowhere today and would have no clue how to reach for the destiny He's designed for us. Do you see that truth in your life? Can you look back at your story and see how God's sovereign hand and power brought you out of the miry clay? There are no dreams to pursue without God's power!

Give Credit Where Credit Is Due

God is not looking for an incredible person to use for His purposes; He's looking for a credible one. You don't need great abilities in order for God to use you for great tasks; you just need to be willing to depend on Him and give credit where credit is due—and the credit for every good thing is always due to God.

What hinders some people is that when they see praise and credit coming, they grab it because it feels so good to be accepted and recognized. I love the ancient Indonesian parable that illustrates this. The parable describes a turtle who flew through the air by biting on a stick carried between two geese. At first, the turtle was thrilled to take flight, but he became increasingly troubled as he heard the comments from onlookers who praised the geese for being so clever. The turtle felt he deserved the credit and praise so he opened his mouth and shouted,

"This was my idea!" I suspect the turtle's flight ended at that point. The point of the parable is that you cannot have both the credit and the best of life. You have to choose between the two.

I've seen a picture of a turtle that met a better fate. The turtle was sitting on top of a fencepost, enjoying a beautiful view. The caption underneath the picture read, "If you see a turtle on a fencepost, you know he had some help." Whenever I think about that image, I am reminded of the many ways I'm just like that turtle. The only reason I'm so blessed today is that I had a lot of help.

That help comes from trying to develop genuine, sincere humility. The Bible teaches, "Humble yourselves in the presence of the Lord, and He will exalt you" (James 4:10). God moves in when people recognize Him as God. He helps those who depend on Him. The greatest benefit of humility is partnership with God. You can trust your wisdom and ability to get yourself a little credit, or you can trust God's partnership to get you His best for your life.

Insights for Inspiration

- The way up to greatness always starts with bending down in humility.

- Difference-makers are humble enough to accept any call from God.

- Jesus is our greatest example of humility.

Verse to Review

"The reward of humility and the fear of the LORD are riches, honor and life" (Prov. 22:4).

Getting Personal

- What humility lessons have you learned recently?

- Which humility "symptoms" do you possess? Which would you like to develop further?

- How might a more genuine humility lead you to a better future?

12

The Never-Ending Adventure

Only those who risk going too far can
possibly find out how far they can go.

T. S. Eliot

D id you know that red king crabs really are among the kings of the
crab family? An adult male may weigh up to twenty-four pounds
and have a leg span as long as five feet. Their habitat is the chilly waters
of the northern Pacific Ocean and the Bering Sea, along the shores of
Japan, Russia, Alaska, and Canada. They have been known to wander
as much as a hundred miles in a year, sometimes traveling as fast as a
mile a day.

That's pretty impressive work for a crab. As they survey the ocean
floor, these cruising crustaceans feast on clams, mussels, snails, worms,
brittle stars, sea stars, sea urchins, sand dollars, barnacles, other crustaceans, fish parts, sponges, and algae. You could say that over their life
span, which can stretch up to three decades, they rule the seas and take
in sights most of us can only imagine.

We also know that the red king crab does not earn its royal life
easily. They hatch in shallow waters as swimming larvae. During their
first few years, the juvenile crabs molt often, undergoing difficult but

necessary body changes each time they break out of their shells. When they reach maturity after four or five years, they molt less often, but the process of change and growth never ends.

This is just the way the process of change and growth should work for you and me. In childhood and adolescence, we learn and grow rapidly as we go through all kinds of developmental changes. Then, as we become adults, the changes slow down a bit—but they never stop. Our lives will be the most fulfilling for us—and have the greatest impact for God—if we continually seek to break away from the last phase of growth and enter into the next one.

Some people believe that God has imagined a single purpose, one important destiny, for their time on earth. I believe that we limit God with that kind of thinking. It seems to me that His plans for us are far richer and more diverse than what can be summed up by a single achievement. The things God will accomplish through us when we're twenty years old will be entirely different than what He does through us when we're forty or fifty or eighty. God will keep using us and our experiences and talents in a variety of ways—as long as we are willing to keep growing and changing.

Building other people up and helping them grow and succeed is one of the things I enjoy most in life. I love advising, recommending, connecting, and promoting people. When those efforts lead to a break-through, I celebrate with that person and feel as good as if I'd done it myself. And when it happens, it reaffirms for me the realization that life can be an adventure filled with never-ending growth and breakthroughs.

It's a bit like the process of climbing Mount Everest. The trek to the summit is not simply a straight-on assault. First comes the long journey to Nepal and to base camp at nearly 18,000 feet. Then there are stops at Camp I (almost 20,000 feet), Camp II (21,300 feet), Camp III (24,500 feet), and Camp IV (26,000 feet). Climbers may spend hours, days, or weeks moving back and forth between the different levels as they acclimate to the high altitudes. Each camp is an achievement of its own, and after assessing the state of their bodies, the weather, and the dangers ahead, many climbers choose to stop where they are and leave the summit for others to attempt.

However, those with the proper preparation, motivation, and opportunity push on. They are willing to risk leaving the relative safety of their tents in order to break through to new heights. These are the people who eventually reach what may have once seemed impossible—at more than 29,000 feet, the summit of Everest.

Are you ready to make a break for it and climb to heights you've only imagined? What will the adventure of your life look like as you leave your old camp behind?

Let's explore some of the possibilities.

Making the Most of Milestones

With every milestone in life comes a choice: *Will I stop here and bask in the glory and comfort of what I've achieved, or will I use this as a step toward whatever God has in mind for me next?* It's natural to want to catch your breath after taking new ground, and sometimes mental, physical, emotional, or spiritual exhaustion means your rest break will need to stretch into weeks, months, or even years. Just remember not to get so comfortable resting that you give up on growth.

For many of us, our milestones look something like this: High school graduation. College and maybe even postgraduate study. The beginning of a career. Marriage. Parenting. Spiritual growth. Relationship growth with a spouse, family, and friends. Career advances. Pursuit of hobbies and other interests. Helping children move out and establish their own lives. Grandchildren. Retirement.

Other milestones are far less enjoyable yet also are part of life: Divorce. Cancer. The death of loved ones. Unemployment. Doubts about faith. Betrayal by a friend.

Whatever milestone you're in or approaching now, it's an opportunity to prayerfully consider if this is a time to rest or a time to intentionally move forward. And if the answer is "rest," don't stop asking! Tomorrow or someday soon, it may be time to build on today's experience and forge into your future.

In his book *Halftime*, entrepreneur Bob Buford helps men and women in the second half of life realize that the game is changing, and they need to take action:

> You do not have the energy you once had. Fresh out of college, you had no problem with the fourteen-hour days and going in to the office on weekends. It was part of your first-half game plan, something almost inevitable if you hoped to succeed. But now you yearn for something more than success.
>
> Then there is the reality of the game itself: The clock is running. What once looked like an eternity ahead of you is now within reach. And while you do not fear the end of the game, you do want to make sure that you finish well, that you leave something behind no one can take away from you. If the first half was a quest for success, the second half is a journey to significance. . . .
>
> Instead of giving up and settling for life on its own terms, you are ready for new horizons, new challenges. You are ready to move from success to significance—to write your own epitaph—daring to believe that what you ultimately leave behind will be more important than anything you could have achieved in the first half of your life.[1]

Do you feel that yearning for significance? If so, it's likely a sign that God is preparing you for another breakout. Whatever your successes or failures in the past, He is ready to use them—and for *you* to use them—to propel you into the next stage of your destiny. Your first and most important step may be your willingness to believe that God still has important and fulfilling plans for you.

The following are just a few examples of women and men who rejected the idea that they were done growing, changing, and contributing. They broke the mold and moved to a new level in life.

- Virginia's Kate Clary had been an elementary school teacher for more than twenty years. Yet she'd always dreamed of serving children in a deeper and more personal way. "As a single mom with two grown biological boys, I realized if I was going to answer this 'call within,' I had better get to it," she said. Kate began the process for international adoption. In 2006, she received the referral of two Guatemalan newborn boys. That same week, a local family asked her if she would take their two-year-old son for the weekend; she eventually adopted him, too. Now in her sixties, Kate is mom to two nine-year-olds and an eleven-year-old, as well as two biological sons in their thirties and two grandchildren. "People shouldn't let their age dictate whether they should follow their dreams," she says. "It's never too late."

- For decades, California's John Corcoran lived with a secret, one shared by millions of Americans. He was a college graduate and had even been a teacher for years, but John read at the level of an elementary school student. After failing to learn how to read in school, John developed a belief that many people struggling with illiteracy would identify with: There was something wrong with him. He had resigned himself to it, though he says he always prayed he would learn. Then one day, at the age of forty-eight, he overheard two women in a checkout line talking about how proud they were of their adult brother for finally learning how to read. It gave John the motivation to go to a reading clinic to get help. In thirteen months, he was reading at a second grade level. Another 125 hours later, he was reading at a twelfth grade level. Since learning to read, John has written poetry, authored books, and started a foundation to provide tutors for students who cannot read. "I used to call my illiteracy a curse," he says, "but now it's a blessing in that I get to encourage others and show it's never too late to learn how to read."

- Vivian Stancil never had an easy time of things. She overcame a rough childhood in the foster care system and at age nineteen, with two small sons at home, lost her vision completely. This unstoppable woman went on to become the first blind teacher in the Long Beach, California, school district. But it was at age fifty that the real test to her spirit came. Her doctor told her that if she didn't lose weight she wouldn't live to see sixty. She cheated death and conquered her own fears by jumping into a swimming pool. Vivian learned to swim and lost more than one hundred pounds. Now the Riverside, California, resident is an accomplished National Senior Games athlete with hundreds of medals. She created the Vivian Stancil Olympian Foundation to help seniors and at-risk youth participate in sports and fitness. "You will always have someone telling you [that] you can't do something," she says. "Just believe in yourself."[2]

- You've probably heard of Henry Winkler, the actor, director, and producer who is probably best known for playing Arthur "The Fonz" Fonzarelli on the old television sitcom *Happy Days*. You may not know that Winkler, now nearly seventy, has embarked on a surprising new career as a children's book author. He is the coauthor of the popular series *Hank Zipzer: The World's Greatest Underachiever*, which tells the adventures of a young boy who has dyslexia. Hank is based on Winkler's own childhood, in which he struggled in school because of his undiagnosed learning disability. "At one time it was so hard for me to read a book. It is so monumental for me to be able to write a book. I want kids to be able to identify, laugh, and realize that they're not alone no matter what their learning challenge is."[3]

What is the secret, unfulfilled dream in your heart? Where do you sense God leading you that you've previously been too afraid to pursue? Now may be exactly the right time to unleash God's power and discover the next step in your destiny.

The Levels of My Life

My own life has been filled with opportunities to shatter the shell I was in, keep growing, and break through to a new level. My breakouts began on the night of my stabbing and my desperate plea to God. I could have given up on life or rejected God's ability to save me, but I had just enough sense to realize that there was only one answer and I had only one chance, which was to ask God for help. It confirmed for me that my best bet was to trust God to guide and plan the rest of my days on earth and into eternity.

When the Lord called me to preach, I questioned for a time if He knew what He was doing. Then He seemed to be calling me to lead a small group of believers at a church called Cascade Hills, which seemed equally strange and unpromising. But the joy and blessings He has bestowed on me and the people of our church over all these years have shown me once again that His plan is best.

After I met and married Debbie, I should have moved into a new stage of growth. But during those first few years of our marriage, I missed out on my destiny. I didn't give Debbie the love and attention that she deserved and that our relationship needed. Fortunately, as you know, God got my attention through the heart-piercing words of another pastor: "If you don't take care of your home life, you don't have anything to say." It was enough to get me back on track.

I have faced opposition in different forms over the years. There were the pastors who shunned me after our church started growing. There was the church financial crisis. In the early days, there was also a small group of men who wanted me to resign as pastor. I took that idea to the congregation, and the people voiced their definite preference for me to stay. It turned out that those men and their families were the ones who ended up leaving. I just wanted to remain in God's will and was grateful He cleared that obstacle away.

I battled another kind of opposition beginning in 2001. I began to experience shortness of breath and noticed I couldn't walk thirty feet without having to stop and rest. So I did what most of us do when we feel sick—I went to the Internet. I found an article entitled "Ten Signs You Are Having a Heart Attack" but after reading it realized I had "only" nine of the ten signs. Being a confident optimist, I told myself, "I'm okay because I don't have sign number six."

Whether it's through trusted family and friends, our experiences, or our own body, God uses a variety of methods to communicate with us and guide us to the next level. But we can't break out of our shell if we're in denial about what we're seeing and hearing, and that's where I was on that day. By the time I finally went to the doctor, I was diagnosed with three arteries that were 90 percent blocked. One of them, known as the "widow maker," was the left anterior descending artery. If closed off completely, I was told, it would cause a massive heart attack that was most often fatal. Doctors put in a series of stents, which had me up and running again in no time.

For some reason, though, my body later rejected the stents. One day, while walking a beach with my son in Florida, I felt a severe pain in my chest and knew something was wrong. I began taking nitroglycerin tablets to get through the weekend. On Monday, my wife and another couple insisted I see a specialist. After I arrived, the doctor declared that I was having a heart attack at that moment and needed bypass surgery immediately.

I thought something must be wrong with God's plan for me. I'd already had my "train wreck" in life when I was stabbed. It was time for someone else to have a crisis, not me again. I reasoned somehow that everyone is assigned one major life crisis that turns them either toward or away from God. It didn't seem fair. I knew people who had never had one serious catastrophe or disaster, and now I was having my second. I thought it was a divine mix-up.

While the hospital staff prepared me for surgery and I exchanged my clothing for a hospital gown, I noticed a Bible lying nearby and picked it up. Words from the book of Isaiah seemed to dance off the page to catch my attention: "When you pass through the waters, I will be with you; and through the rivers, they will not overflow you. When you walk through the fire, you will not be scorched, nor will the flame burn you. For I am the LORD your God. . . . Do not fear, for I am with you" (Isa. 43:2–5). A sudden peace came over me that I could not explain.

After triple bypass surgery, I woke up in a recovery room. Once I'd gathered my senses, I couldn't help but thank God again for His mercy and grace. Through my close call, He'd reminded me how precious life is. Each new day for me became a gift, not a guarantee. When we view life this way it helps us prioritize better. My heart attack helped me decide to give my best to the people who will cry the deepest at my funeral. I'd always loved my family, but experiences like this made me appreciate them, others, and God even more.

That's my story so far—a series of opportunities to discover the lessons God has wanted me to learn. Though I've had missteps along the way, I've tried to trust Him at each point. Whenever I did, His amazing love and power allowed me to break through to the next level. It's been a grand adventure, and I can't wait to see what happens next.

Your story will look entirely different from mine because God has a unique plan for each of us. What I do know is that yours can be surprising, exciting, and fulfilling if you put God in charge. He's the One with the divine blueprint, and you can be sure that He's ready to use you to build something special.

It's also important to remember that whether you're eighteen or eighty, you're never too young or too old to get back on the path that God is guiding you toward. I was once asked to officiate at the wedding of a young woman named Diane. About thirty minutes before the ceremony was supposed to start, she asked to see me. She wore a beautiful wedding dress, but the look on her face didn't match the festive occasion.

"Pastor," she said in a shaky voice, "I've got to tell you something. I'm scared to death. He's highly abusive. He's tried to choke me. He's threatened me. My family doesn't know, nobody knows, but he's violent. Everything in me is saying don't go through with this, but I'm so ashamed. If I call the wedding off, I'll let everybody down. What do I do?"

"Diane, listen," I said. "If you go through with this, every step you take down that aisle, you're going to be asking yourself, 'What am I doing?' It's like the Green Mile. You're going to be walking to your own death. If you stop the wedding, you're going to temporarily feel some embarrassment. But if I were you, I wouldn't go through with it."

Through tears, she said, "I'm not going through with it."

While Diane talked to her parents and brother about what was happening and why, I pulled the groom aside and told him the game was up. He didn't deny what Diane had said. I explained that in a few minutes, Diane's father and brother were going to come looking for him and that it wouldn't be pleasant. He took off. Then I addressed the wedding guests: "Folks, you won't understand why right now, but they want to call the wedding off, and there's a good reason for it. I know this is an inconvenience, and if any of you want your gifts back, they'd be more than happy to return them. I don't want you to walk away disappointed or wondering what's wrong. This could be the best decision ever for both their lives."

A couple of years later, I received a letter from Diane. She thanked me for my help that day and said she'd married a wonderful man who treated her with such respect and love that she couldn't believe how close she came to missing out on it all. Her difficult decision on her almost–wedding day was the big breakthrough that changed her life for the better.

It's okay to admit that you've taken a detour from your destiny. You can't turn around until you're first honest with yourself. From there, it's important to remember that God is more interested in getting you back on track than punishing you for your mistakes. Yes, getting back to God's plan may be difficult or embarrassing. You may feel like you're letting someone down. But the truth is that none of that matters much. Our task is to fulfill the purposes that God has in store for us. Anytime we're not moving in that direction, it's time for a course correction, no matter how old we are and no matter what the circumstances.

Sticking with the Basics

We all hope that as we move down the road in this journey called life, we'll grow in wisdom and maturity. Ideally, each stage of growth takes us deeper into our faith and closer to the person we were created to be. There's a danger that accompanies all that growth, however. We can begin to think that we've "arrived" and that we don't need to worry anymore about the fundamentals.

One of the privileges I've had in ministry is seeing the progress of people who have a big dream, work hard for it, stay focused, and now live out what they always wanted. One of these is professional baseball's Tim Hudson. When Tim was in college, a friend invited him to our church. He made some spiritual decisions at that time that helped anchor his direction in life. I still remember the excitement in his voice on the day he phoned to tell me he'd been called up to pitch in the big leagues for the Oakland A's. What a moment!

Since that time, I also watched Tim play for the Atlanta Braves and San Francisco Giants. He had an amazing career that spanned seventeen years and included four All-Star Game appearances. Every time I saw Tim pitch, I observed the same passion for the game that he had when he first started out.

What's interesting about professional baseball is that each year all the players spend weeks in spring training going over the basics of throwing, batting, and catching. They just keep honing the basic skills relentlessly. You'd think that the pros wouldn't need to do this. Even though they know the game's fundamentals and execute them better than anyone, they tirelessly work on perfecting them until the season begins.

There's a lesson in that for all of us. No matter how long you've lived the Christian life or how far you've ascended in position or prestige, you'll never be so spiritual that you won't have to keep mastering the basics of praying, reading the Bible, and spending time with God. You'll never be so mature or lofty that you won't have to face temptations. Lust of the flesh, pride, jealousy, greed, and hatred are still just as dangerous—and perhaps more so—as we grow. As you put into practice some of the ideas you've found in this book, I hope you'll remember to continue practicing the basics.

I'm trying to do that as I move ahead in my own life. I don't want to be distracted by temptations. My aim is to stay focused on God's plan for my future. A famous tightrope walker was once asked, "What is the key to walking on the tightrope? You make it look so easy."

He answered, "The secret is to keep your eyes fixed on where you are going. You never look down. Where your head goes, that's where your body is going too. If you look down, there's a good chance you will fall. So you always have to look to where you want to be."[4]

That's good advice. It's what we've been talking about throughout the pages of this book. Don't allow your gaze to rest on current circumstances and what's holding you back. Focus instead on the goals and destination that God has planted in your heart. The more you practice looking ahead, the easier it will be the next time, and the more you will grow into your destiny.

Insights for Inspiration

- Our lives will be the most fulfilling for us—and have the greatest impact for God—if we continually seek to break away from the last phase of growth and enter into the next one.

- A yearning for significance is a likely sign that God is preparing you for another breakout.

- You're never too young or too old to get back on the path that God is guiding you toward.

Verse to Review

*"Behold, I will do something new, now it will spring forth;
will you not be aware of it? I will even make a roadway
in the wilderness, rivers in the desert"* (Isa. 43:19).

Getting Personal

- What are the breakout events in your life? What did you learn and in what ways did you grow in those times?

- When have you missed opportunities to break through to a new level of growth? Why was that?

- What breakthrough or next level of growth do you sense God may be calling you to next?

Epilogue

I'm sure you remember from the beginning of this book the story of my stabbing and miraculous recovery. Do you also remember the light pole I held on to while dying and praying to God?

What I haven't told you is that every April 28 since, I've gone back to that spot, knelt by the same pole, and thanked God for His mercy and salvation. I've been doing that now since 1975. It might be raining, or cold, or late in the evening, but I still find a way to get there. Once I was scheduled to speak from April 27 to 29 at an event in Dallas, Texas. On the morning of the twenty-eighth, I flew from Dallas to Atlanta, caught a connecting flight to Columbus, took a taxi to the light pole, prayed while the driver kept the engine running, then flew back to Dallas so I could speak again that night.

Not long ago, I received an interesting phone call from the CEO of Columbus Regional Medical Center, the same hospital where I nearly died. He told me that the hospital had bought the property where "my" light pole stood and would soon be demolishing the area. He'd heard, however, how important that light pole was to me. "Would you like to have it?" he asked.

"Absolutely!" I said.

We arranged to have it taken to Cascade Hills. Since that time, over a dozen volunteers stepped up to create a beautiful stone prayer garden for people to enjoy, with that very same light pole in the center. It includes an inscription that reads, "Under this light on April 28, 1974, our pastor cried out to God in desperation for a miracle that saved his soul and life. Perhaps your prayers to God in desperation today will be answered with the miracle you need."

I keep going back to that pole because I can't get away from the story in the Bible about the ten lepers Jesus healed. Nine of them never thanked Him, but one did. I want to be the one who never forgets what He's done for me. Each year, I pray and thank God for the young man who had the courage to knock on my front door and plant a spiritual seed, for the skill of the doctors and nurses, and most of all for God's gift of new life to an undeserving teenager.

God wants you to have a new life, too—the incredible, fulfilling life that He imagined specifically for you. You are not doomed to repeat your mistakes. Your past does not need to define your future. Don't wait for a crisis or wake-up call before you begin seeking the life you were meant for. Dare to break free of your shell and discover the amazing, God-directed life that is so much more than you can dream of.

As you break through the barriers and discover God's best for your life, I hope you never lose a sense of wonder over the journey. I once went to Israel with my marriage mentor, A. T. Stewart. We had a blast. We didn't know anyone in our group of about thirty travelers, who were from all over the United States. On the first day, A. T. yelled out, "Bill, can you believe we're here, just two ol' Georgia boys standing at the Wailing Wall in Jerusalem?" Everyone smiled at the innocent comment. Later on our tour, A. T.'s loud voice rang out again: "Bill, can you believe we're here, just two ol' Georgia boys at the Garden of Gethsemane?"

By the time we got to the Jordan River, half of our group was joining in when A. T. launched into his predictable announcements. On the last day of the trip, A. T. started up again: "Bill—" Before he could finish, the rest of our group roared, "Can you believe we're here, just two ol' Georgia boys at the empty tomb of Jesus?"

My final wish for you is that you know God the way I do. I'd love for you to join in with us one day in heaven, when A. T. yells out, "Bill, can you believe we're here, just two ol' Georgia boys in this place called heaven?"

Every breakthrough and every challenge in life will bring us closer to our purpose. Yet our final destiny and destination is with God in the place He's prepared for us. That's the joyful result of God's plan for you, the final breakthrough. It's the home where you belong.

If I don't meet you before then, I can't wait to see you there.

Notes

Chapter 2: Uniquely You

1. Rita Sutton, "A Mother's Love," *Knoxville Journal*, May 11, 2012, http://theknoxvillejournal.com/a-mothers-love/.

Chapter 3: Breaking Free

1. C. S. Lewis, *Mere Christianity* (New York: Macmillan, 1953), 159.
2. Lori Mangrum, "I Was Panic-Stricken," *Today's Christian Woman*, http://www.todayschristianwoman.com/articles/1997/september/7w5050.html.
3. Pete Wilson, Twitter message.

Chapter 4: Dressing for Destiny

1. Urijah Faber, Twitter message.

Chapter 5: Envisioning Your Future

1. Thomas D. Schneid, *Creative Safety Solutions* (Boca Raton: CRC Press, 1998), 93.
2. Walt Kallestad, *Wake Up Your Dreams* (Grand Rapids: Zondervan, 1996).
3. Michelle Tauber, "Author Kathryn Stockett Giving a Voice to 'The Help,'" *People*, August 22, 2011, http://www.people.com/people/archive/article/0,,20523320,00.html; Jeremy Kingsley, *Inspired People Produce Results* (New York: McGraw-Hill Education, 2013), 106–7.
4. James Risen, "Prince of Pizza," *Los Angeles Times*, October 11, 1987, http://articles.latimes.com/1987–10–11/business/fi-13386_1_pizza-hut.

5. "History of CPYR," Crystal Peaks Youth Ranch website, http://www
   .crystalpeaksyouthranch.org/about-cpyr/history-of-cpyr/.
6. Spanx website, http://www.spanx.com/about-us; Clare O'Conner,
   "Spanx Inventor Sara Blakely on Hustling Her Way to a Billion-Dollar
   Business," *Forbes*, October 21, 2014, http://www.forbes.com/sites/
   clareoconnor/2014/10/21/spanx-inventor-sara-blakely-on-hustling-her
   -way-to-a-billion-dollar-business/.
7. Peb Jackson and James Lund, *Danger Calling* (Grand Rapids: Revell,
   2010), 87–93.
8. "Florence Chadwick 1953–1964," *Queen of the Channel*, http://www
   .queenofthechannel.com/florence-chadwick.

Chapter 6: Faith over Fear

1. Austin Carr, "Risky Innovation: Will Starbucks's Leap of Faith
   Pay Off?" *Fast Company*, http://www.fastcompany.com/3009040/
   risky-innovation-will-starbuckss-leap-of-faith-pay-off.
2. Lee Strobel, *God's Outrageous Claims* (Grand Rapids: Zondervan, 1997),
   199–200.
3. Dr. Ben Carson, *Take the Risk* (Grand Rapids: Zondervan, 2008), 105.

Chapter 7: The End of Excuses

1. Frank Shamrock and Charles Fleming, *Uncaged: My Life as a Champion
   MMA Fighter* (Chicago: Chicago Review Press, 2012).
2. Dennis Kizziar, *Hope for the Troubled Heart* (Bend, Ore: Maverick
   Publications, 2008), 35–36.
3. Kizziar, *Hope for the Troubled Heart*, 47–48.
4. Dallas Willard, *The Spirit of the Disciplines: Understanding How God
   Changes Lives* (San Francisco: HarperOne, 1999), 120.
5. Kimberlee Conway Ireton, "Telling the Truth," *A Deeper Story* website,
   July 5, 2013, http://deeperstory.projects.cacpro.com/telling-the-truth/.

Chapter 8: Strength from Within

1. Tim Kimmel, *Little House on the Freeway* (Portland, Ore.: Multnomah, 1987), 67–70.
2. Peb Jackson and James Lund, *Danger Calling* (Grand Rapids: Revell, 2010), 40–45.
3. Thomas Jefferson and Thomas FitzHugh, *Letters of Thomas Jefferson Concerning Philology and the Classics* (Charleston: Nabu Press, 2010), 42.
4. Cynthia Barnett, "Is Cheating Becoming a Way of Life?" *The News & Observer*, November 2, 1997, section 1, page 5. Also see "Losing a Racquetball Game," https://isharesps.org/websitedoc/CharacterEd/Integrity-Children.pdf.

Chapter 9: Choose Your Mentors Well

1. Wolfgang Bauder, *"tapeinophrosyne,"* *The New International Dictionary of New Testament Theology*, vol. 2, ed. Colin Brown (Grand Rapids: Zondervan, 1976, 1986), 259, 263.

Chapter 10: Coping with Critics

1. Phil McGraw, *Life Code* (Los Angeles: Bird Street Books, 2012), 92.
2. H. Jackson Brown, quoted in John C. Maxwell, *Your Roadmap for Success Workbook* (Nashville: Thomas Nelson, 2002), 146.

Chapter 11: The Way Up Is Down

1. Andrew Murray, quoted in Roy B. Zuck, *The Speaker's Quotebook* (Grand Rapids: Kregel Publications, 1997, 2009), 269.
2. C. S. Lewis, quoted in Wayne Martindale and Jerry Root, *The Quotable Lewis* (Wheaton, Ill.: Tyndale House, 1989), 495.
3. Phillips Brooks, quoted in Norman H. Drummond, *True Humility* (Bloomington, Ind.: WestBow Press, 2012), 115.
4. Edward K. Rowell, *Fresh Illustrations for Preaching and Teaching* (Grand Rapids: Baker, 1997), 206.
5. Martin Luther, quoted in Mary Ann Jeffreys, "Colorful Sayings of

Colorful Luther," *Christianity Today*, April 1, 1992, http://www
.christianitytoday.com/ch/1992/issue34/3427.html.
6. Alice Gray, *Stories for the Heart: The Second Collection* (Sisters, Ore.:
Multnomah, 2001), 105.
7. Abraham Lincoln, "Abraham Lincoln Quotes," *HistoryNet* website,
http://www.historynet.com/abraham-lincoln-quotes.

Chapter 12: The Never-Ending Adventure

1. Bob Buford, *Halftime* (Grand Rapids: Zondervan, 1994), 20–21.
2. "50 After 50: The Risk Takers," *Huffington Post*, August 4, 2014, http://
www.huffingtonpost.com/2014/08/04/50-over-50-the-risk-taker_n_
5639797.html?1407149439.
3. "Biography: Henry Winkler," *Scholastic*, http://www.scholastic.com/
teachers/contributor/henry-winkler.
4. Joel Osteen, *Become a Better You* (Brentwood, Tenn.: Howard, 2009), 11.

billpurvis
LEADERSHIP

Are you ready to

MAKE A BREAK FOR IT

in your life?

I invite you to join
BILL PURVIS LEADERSHIP
for monthly inspiration! Take the
next step towards the life you desire.
Monthly Subscriptions are only
$15 A MONTH.

This opportunity and additional
resources can be found at
BILLPURVIS.COM.

Westminster Public Library
3705 W. 112th Ave.
Westminster, CO 80031
www.westminsterlibrary.org